LOOKIN' FOR JOY

LOOKIN' FOR JOY

BETH GOOBIE

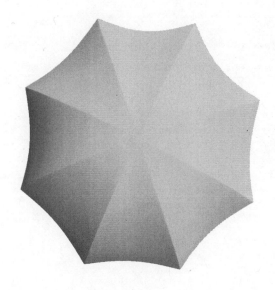

singular fiction, poetry, nonfiction, translation, drama, and graphic books

Library and Archives Canada Cataloguing in Publication

Title: Lookin' for joy / Beth Goobie.
Other titles: Looking for joy
Names: Goobie, Beth, 1959- author.
Description: Poems.
Identifiers: Canadiana (print) 20220180563 | Canadiana (ebook) 2022018058X |
ISBN 9781550969771 (softcover) | ISBN 9781550969788 (EPUB) |
ISBN 9781550969795 (Kindle) | ISBN 9781550969801 (PDF)
Classification: LCC PS8563.O8326 L66 2022 | DDC C811/.54—dc23

We gratefully acknowledge the Canada Council for the Arts,
the Government of Canada, the Ontario Arts Council, and
Ontario Creates for their support toward our publishing activities.

Canadian sales representation: The Canadian Manda Group,
664 Annette Street, Toronto ON M6S 2C8.
www.mandagroup.com 416 516 0911

North American and international distribution, and U.S. sales:
Independent Publishers Group, 814 North Franklin Street,
Chicago IL 60610 www.ipgbook.com toll free: 1 800 888 4741

for the *Tonight It's Poetry* crowd
Sundays, 8 p.m., Amigos Cantina, Saskatoon
(funded by SK Arts)
Slam on!

At the Mic

The Civilization Inside My Head

The other day I got a phone call in one of my lower left molars.
It was a girl from Sudbury, asking for Justin Bieber.
I told her she had the wrong cavity.
Have you ever noticed how the voices in your head
tend to sound like Charles Manson's disciples?
It's never the Dalai Lama popping in for a mantra,
never Deepak Chokra wanting to discuss butterfly hurricanes,
or Leonard Cohen, back from the dead, to hum a little "Hallelujah."
It's as if Bell Telephone has strung a party line
from my left temple to my right,
and all of the afternoon soap opera addicts
are sending me telepathic commentaries on their favourite shows.
Or I get a direct line to the Osmonds singing hyperdrive
so they sound like they've got Yuletide chipmunks stuck in their throats.
Alternate universes have hooked up a high-speed InterOptic cable
behind my right eye; they google me day and night.
Alien computer systems track my every thought,
then they analyse my Neanderthal potential.
If only the Big Bang inside my mind would reverse itself:
Suck it up, Brain. Suck all that sonic junk back into the void.

But that begs the question: without the noise inside our heads,
would we exist? Without that non-stop high-school cafeteria mayhem
skateboarding along our corpus callosums,
could we stake a claim to civilization?
Do we really want to go back to a pan flute
puffing cumulonimbus across serene sapphire blue
while sheep safely graze? Aren't you twitching

for the remote to turn on the prowling wolf?
We've all been occupied. The Fathers of Confederation
wrote each of us as a clause into the British North America Act,
and there's a railroad blasting shore to shore
across the continent of our dreaming.
If you can get that train to slow down,
hop on board and visit the passengers.
They'll tell you about the hell holes they've crawled out of,
the choirs of angels that vibrate their craniums,
the White House tweets that keep jamming their collective anus.
Civilization is constipated with contact,
but you never know when Horton will hear the next Who.
Right now, Dr. Seuss could be phoning one of your wisdom teeth.
You don't want to miss that call.

The Girl with the Origami Soul

When the world sits on your face, stop smiling and bite,
says the girl with the origami soul. Leave a good impression.
You're no snowflake, exquisite with holes poked into you by mean queens.
Expectations are a cookie cutter that won't turn *you* into dessert.
There's always another way out, says back door girl.
When reality flattens you to two dimensions, refold into crawling worm,
I'm-outta-here heartbeat, afterlove laughter that blows through any barbed-wire fence.
Your perimeters are my goodbye, says astronaut girl, says shadow girl,
says slinky-down-the-stairs-and-out-of-your-prayers hiss girl.
You chewed me up and spat me out, a soft oozing rumour that, years later,
still fuses to the bottom of your shoe, tracking you everywhere you go –
a footprint face who refuses to live as small as your hatred.
I twisted out of your mind games, says pretzel girl.
I resurrected off your bedroom altar, says penis angel girl.
Anyone can be broken down to base intentions, and that's all you thought I was –
one of your intentions, stripped of its orgasms and stored in that smug afterlife
where you keep all your good little spank girls.

But I learned a long time ago not to live in the good, says snake oil girl.
Bad is where you lose obligation like your reflection in a mirror
when the candle snuffs and you're left with death in your mouth.
Swallow it down, feel what it's like to live with the end
of every witch way you knew yourself,
that sorcery of a revolving mirror ball of faces.
You don't have to be a guru to know maya is just another word
for drinking the poison of now in the hope of escaping the toxin of tomorrow.
That either kills you or forces a tolerance, says phoenix girl.
It's the one who chooses to drink the venom of herself

who learns to break illusion down to *the* base assumption,
the narcotic that you'll survive by offering yourself up in small bites.
Rehab means you stop worshipping your tooth marks.
Where's the joy in missing pieces? says jigsaw girl.
Once you fit them all together, the picture starts to move.

The small Big

The Big small wants you to spend your life dancing on the prick of a pin.
Lower your gaze, hunch your shoulders, endure repetitive thought injury
that locks you into a negative universe and anti-matter. *Let there be darkness ...*
a looooooong dark tunnel with a far-off pinprick of light, calling you to dance
the same old pain. The Big small knows we're all squares in a Rubik's cube,
each of us responsible for fitting into the required pattern. And the pattern
is beautiful – see how you've been woven into exquisite stasis.
You know who you are – that note there, liquid in the trumpet's bell,
always fourth in the melodic run that peaks in such diminished harmony.
Or you're a nail invisible in the cathedral ceiling, the one that keeps
every oak beam, every stained-glass window, every kneeling worshipper in place.
At least that's what the Big small told you as it hammered you into position.
But sometimes, as you're up there dancing on your own nail prick,
you can't help wondering what a little origami could do to all this obedience –
add a serpent to the garden, a door to a concrete wall, a pilgrimage
toward choice that would finally get you up off your knees.
That thought lights you up like a single lavender square –
deviant in a Rubik's cube gone rogue – and suddenly you're small Big,
a lotus playing origami with your crown as it opens you to a positive universe.
The Big small wants to suck you on its tongue like a Lifesaver
that freshens its breath as you dissolve to sweet nothing,
but the small Big knows the chance to dance on the enemy's tongue
is the moment truth pulls the lie out of the cathedral ceiling
and possibility begins its slow unfold out of the rubble where we're all small
questions looking for a way to ask ourselves alive.

How to Make an Angel Giggle

The difference between human and angel is one chromosome
and the minor complaint of flesh. But it is flesh that can laugh
and angels can only judge. The foreheads of celestials gleam
as if lit by stern light bulbs, whereas humans frolic among lilac hedges
and blossoming shadow, their nerve tips opening small white flowers.
A woman smiles to say come hither, an angel snorts fire and brimstone.
Seraphim converse in telepathic lightning that staggers humans to their knees,
eyes begging the apocalyptic sky for clues to their future,
but archangels live at the speed of light and the future is a cosmic myth
they leave to those who wish upon stars they think are still there.
Pious grandmothers believe cherubim descend into the tick-tock of their lives
to hover over teacup doilies and hand-deliver their prayers.
They know angels email themselves across the Milky Way in the seconds
it takes a teenage grandson to recognize himself in the morning mirror;
by the time the kiddo sits down to eat his Choco Puffs,
angels have dined on anti-matter and visited several black holes.

Principalities and dominions vibrate at exalted frequencies
that occasionally download another archetype or a new world order;
tuned to the divine, they rarely pick up on human static.
But fallen angels can be pulled into the buzz.
These angels love to boost, can't resist the charge they get
latched onto a proton sparking the nucleus of a human molecule –
be it in the brain, the big toe, the liver, or the clitoris, this joy ride
guarantees an angel the subatomic giggles, shared in good faith
with any demons hooting it up on counterbalancing electrons.
Humans unwittingly transformed into a molecular fairground
find themselves bubbling with laughter, accompanied by the sorts of visions

one would expect of rebellious lucifers, getting their kicks
inside kidneys and colons. All that mirth gets inside their chromosomes,
tweaking the angel, tweaking the demon, tweaking the guffawing human
into a hybrid species that travels the giggle toward immortality
and doesn't care if it ever arrives.

The Piano at the Centre of the Universe

There is a piano at the centre of the universe –
a small lit stage that vibrates on the tip of God's nose.
Every song sung, every tavern tune and hymn,
the laments of meteors travelling their frozen circuits,
the curious hum of earthworms as they nose through the underfoot –
from the collapsed sonics of a black hole to the choirs of heaven,
all first notes emanate from this keyboard.
The pianist hunched over the cosmic Steinway
wears a sequined bodysuit, platform shoes and gender
that slipslides like Big Bang jazz. Those manicured hands converse
with semitones and overtones, the harmonics of ancestral spirits,
the imagination of D#, the moods of B. Chromosomal sequences tinkle,
an affectionate triad materializes the platypus,
a backfiring chord rolls out the Volkswagen Beetle.
The Milky Way shimmers, a high octave played in a house of mirrors,
segues into a show-stopping overture that ushers in an alien invasion,
and Neanderthals learn the chord called human.

Sometimes the pianist seems to be composing wormholes
that travel directly through God's cerebrum,
and divine altered states split infinity
into the longest reggae riff ever to groove possibility.
The piano at the centre of the universe is no moralist, doesn't select
which of God's vibes to hum and howl toward manifestation,
and once the frequency is sent out no echo travels back,
though the pianist occasionally weeps as a long moan reverberates –
perhaps a species going extinct or a planet knocked out of orbit.
What do you understand of the material plane

when you and your piano are but a wave form improvising
in that higher state of utter genesis, only the orgasmic bliss of creation,
no resistance or consequence, no aftermath within time. Although
the piano at the centre of the universe is actually a piano within time –
a metaphor in a poem that vibrates on the tip of a poet's nose
who rarely manifests orgasmic bliss, but then all divinely inspired wave forms
must ultimately descend into the physical dimension
where yellow taxis don't freestyle in and out of dandelions and lollipops,
unless, of course, they end up in a poem as human as this one.

The Reader

The reader's psyche is dusty and crumb-ridden, and always dwells in an attic.
Bookcases insulate the walls, keeping out boredom, every shelf lined three deep.
Cobwebs slumber in corners, dreaming intricate plots for themselves;
the reader considers a cobweb a pet and needs nothing further,
except a bed, two plumped pillows, and a side table for a mug of tea.
A cat with a literary purr may be permitted;
bats that flap in and out of consciousness are ignored.
The reader can hear conversation pitched higher than a bat's;
the whisper of waiting story hovers dense as incense,
the air hypnotic with characters calling for their lives to open and begin.
In this way, the reader knows she is tenebrously accompanied.
Candle-shadow shelters the gargoyle that reads over her shoulder;
angels flicker at her temples, trying to follow her thoughts.
When she reads aloud, words resound like ancient cities in her mouth,
cobblestoned and crowded with hurly-burly and scramble.

For the reader embodies entire civilizations. Though she embraces solitude,
she contains a rabbit warren bustling with come-and-go personas –
a talking frog hurtles a motorcar through her chest,
a suffragette sets fire to history in her bowels,
a child flees a residential school in the tears that teach her eyes.
An inkling can summon the reader on an interdimensional pilgrimage;
a mad chronology of verbs takes her in and out of metaphor,
the howl of vowels prowls her along the cliff edge of transformation,
altered states open her like a Japanese fan.
The reader lives inside the perpetual request to be changed,
and the mind that sighs a book closed is always a world richer
than the one that hoped it open. Between metamorphoses,

the reader rests her chin on a clammy windowsill, gazing out
into rainy epics that are stories telling themselves to the air
before they soak into ground and river, myths of the earth
drunk deep by all her children. The reader knows
she swallows heaven and beyond in a glass of water, other realms
that have agreed to take up residence in her molecules
and spin new ideas around the thinker in each cell.
The reader's very chromosomes are an alphabet inviting in new letters,
her flesh a language that invents itself through dialogue,

and when she offers to lend you her favourite book,
understand that with the first word, you will not be the same.

In Praise of the Gloomy Day

Mood with her pencil, sketching the day charcoal, its kingdoms of cloud.
Rain like a Beethoven sonata, a Brahms ballade that forks lighting
through bone. Gloom collects in house corners, under backyard trees,
such a rich darkness, it always makes you feel deep in your skin
as if you contained an inner cave system, an underground civilization
that gathers around midnight bonfires to mythologize the first echo.
Flesh murmurs and mutters. Small gargoyles have taken up residence
in your nooks and crannies; they hold subatomic conversations
about crossroad omens, the snobbery of angels.
You could take your own sketchbook and materialize crumbling doorways,
their beckoning shadowy interiors, the reflection you always wished
would appear in your bedroom mirror. Gloomy afternoons summon
forgotten stories you used to tell about yourself –
there, by the window, the girl who could fly like a black wind;
on the couch, the teenager scribbling a treasury of smart-ass comebacks;
on the table, the poisoned apple of love and the knowing vixen
who was never going to bite. All the fairy tales are yours on gloomy days,
every room replete with your own fables walking toward you –
the Green Man slyly entwined with wild ivy desire,
an old hag dressed in a lifetime of pockets. She empties them
as she hobbles, and you could scavenge for wisdom in her wake,
examine each cast-off trinket, dense and weighted as a heart
that finally realizes it has wasted its life on all the wrong things,

or you could let the November rain charcoal you stark, stripped-down –
a maple tree unadorned yet exquisite with change of mind,
each branch heading off into a myriad of choices,
a jumbled ecstasy of tiny pencils, each dreaming
another shadowy interior, asking to be sketched into whim.

Why I Love the Accordion

The accordion wears sensible shoes and loud paisley ties.
It waddles like a pug and smokes Cuban cigars.
If it floated, it would be a tugboat.
The accordion answers the door in a housecoat, its hair in curlers.
It'll wear a kiss of lipstick, but decries cosmetic surgery
as an STD caught by those who make love to mirrors.
The accordion plays checkers like it's coming into style.
It's as happy square-dancing in a church basement
as downing a tavern pint, and it always waltzes the moon home.
The accordion can get lonely. Love plays it in a minor key
like a young mustached woman in a sleeveless yellow dress.
Toss it your bread crumbs; it watches you with a pigeon's eye,
discerning the tourist from the elderly woman in slippers
who tells the story of her life in coos and clucks.

The accordion reads detective stories and graphic novels,
and doesn't know how to spell Nietzsche.
At a child's birthday party, it wears a pointed hat and blindfold
as it pins the tail on the donkey. After the party's over,
the accordion sits in a late-night kitchen, trying to figure out
how to pay the kids' dental bills. With a sigh, it tells itself
wealth is a breath of air that flows through open windows;
the rest is just money you lock up in a bank.
The accordion has its troubles, but it hides them.
At 40, it gains 10 pounds and takes up belly dancing.
It has been known to introduce itself with "I'm just a fat old guy"
and a smile that sets church bells ringing; the accordion believes
civilization begins with the way we greet each other.
And it knows everyone's hoping; it feels your prayers

like a flock of doves lifting off the Vatican roof,
so that when the accordion sits on a street corner
and opens its tender heart, passersby hum themselves
note by note into a song that brings us all home.

Conversations

I want to live by a cool clear stream under a conversation of blue.
I'd sit on the stoop of my one-room house and listen to the way blue talked to me,
what it had to say about living the day with what the wind blows your way.
The top of your skull dissolves, light kisses your brain direct,
and all the mutter-moods, the dark feeding butterflies disperse.
An inner body opens up then, or another mind arises out of the nerves
speaking their transparent words you can't hear but sense like tiny windows
proclaiming the beyond. The beyond can feel like a kindred spirit,
like Joy whistling along the horizon in gumboots and a floppy straw hat,
carrying its rucksack of pain. Story is: Joy met up with the Devil at a crossroads,
and the Devil tried to win that rucksack in a high-stakes game.
But Joy refused to play, said without pain it got off on itself like a narcotic,
thought it was gonna live forever. There's something about carrying your own pain
that lets your soul know it's loved for the now,
and loved souls stay close, can see the Devil is another worm feeder
dressed in sweet talkin' mendacity – the kind you hear passing your lips
when you've lost touch with your better blue self. Slow down and listen
to the train whistles travelling the distance in your blood.
Train whistles are another way of talking, the four notes of loneliness
that play the inner ache as if they know everything about you,
you're a song that could step out of your life and ride the rails
toward the promise of someone else. That's your composure leaving you
for a minor chord under a prairie sky, and the slow heartbeat of stars
that calls the night sky down into the firmament of your body
so you can feel the moons of your longing orbit your heart
and learn the white silence of their names. Silence can be pure
conversation that trudges Joy over the horizon, whistling to its rucksack
companion chosen for a lifetime of sweet walkin' serendipity;
sometimes pain can talk you on a journey that begins you.

If I Were an Astronaut's Love Child

If I were an astronaut's love child,
the cosmos would consecrate me with deep space DNA.
Stars would spin light years into my molecules
and spellbound planets orbit my heart,
Jupiter trailed by trumpet blasts, Saturn by a discord of crows,
Venus and Mars quarrelling over my affections.
Everywhere I touched, I would leave small moons –
waxing, waning, depending upon my mood.
At the slightest sign of boredom, a wormhole could be summoned.
It is likely I would make a flighty conversationalist.

If I were an astronaut's love child,
I would know the earth from afar –
a great blue heartbeat suspended in longing.
I would not be fooled by day, the way it closes down the sky
and lights up the illusion that this world has it made,
has won the lottery of oxygen, hydrogen and carbon,
perfect distance from the sun. An astronaut's love child
knows everything orbits something else –
prayers on a Ferris wheel lit up against the night sky,
the fairground a galaxy spread out below,
the astronaut's love child in the highest seat,
wrapped in her astronaut mother's arms
as together they ride their heartbeats,
suspended in whimsy that has them hobnobbing with stars,
old friends of the great inner sky.

Painting Mrs. Demerais

Thunder embroiders the afternoon air
outside the Evening Calm Senior's Residence
as 15-year-old volunteer Julie kneels
before Mrs. Demerais, chin pondering its octogenarian chest.
A row of small bottles stands beside the wheelchair.
"I brought them all, like you asked," says Julie.
She unscrews a lid, eases out a damp brush.
"I always thought green was the first colour.
My dad says red, like heartbeat, like blood.
But there was grass here before us,
and I've seen water that looked emerald."
The brush glides across Mrs. Demerais' left large toenail,
describes a tiny farmyard onto its ridged surface.
Mrs. Demerais' chin rises a watching inch.
"Now yellow," says Julie. "Yellow umbrellas make me happy."
She unscrews another lid and paints joy
onto Mrs. Demerais' right large toenail;
bright enough to recall dancing.
Sparks jitterbug across Mrs. Demerais' gaze.
"Elvis," she murmurs, slow in her throat.
"We were all crazy for Elvis."
Julie surveys her waiting bottles, uncaps scarlet.
"For Elvis," she proclaims, and blood heat struts
across the left second toe. "What about Mick?"

Mrs. Demerais snorts; her chin lifts into memory.
"Orange," she replies. "There was a Mustang
that took me driving south of Yorkton.

It was all orange – the car, the sun melting as it went down,
the windowshield so lit up you couldn't look.
His arm in the open window." "Your husband?" asks Julie.
"No," says Mrs. Demerais, chin sinking.
"Derrick was a solid blue. That's all he ever was."
Julie negotiates between past and present.
"I'll put him on the other foot. Is there a story for purple?"
She enriches the third right toenail
as Mrs. Demerais remembers gooseberry-stained chortles,
pies that sweetened her children's mundane.
"And there was another sweetness," she warbles,
chin ascending. "On the Sunday School committee – Netty.
She wore a lovely pink dress." Mrs. Demerais' eyes close,
she hums softly. "Sometimes, sometimes not."
Julie considers the anticipating toenails, opens the pink.
"I'll put Netty beside the Mustang," she decides.
Mrs. Demerais hums Netty and the Mustang over the horizon;
then, in the evening calm, her chin rises one last time.
"There has to be a colour for the bull shit,"
she declares, her gaze a pale glare.
"They want you to believe, and none of it's real.
Remember that, girl – *none* of it's real.
You gotta make it all up for yourself."

Two women stare across the century
that could divide or mirror them,
then Julie holds up a bottle of sparkle-glitter.
"You got it," Mrs. Demerais nods.

Julie paints the gold-glitter next to solid-blue Derrick.
"All I've got left is silver," she sighs,
stroking it onto the left little toe. "Silver for moonlight,
peace and quiet, the chrome on my dad's car
after I've washed it and everything's dripping glad.
The end of the dirt." She chuckles. "The end of bullshit.
I'll paint it onto *both* your pinkies."
She glances up, sees Mrs. Demerais' eyes have closed,
her head slumped sideways, her mouth odd with emptiness.
And within her own warm breathing, Julie knows
Mrs. Demerais has vacated the palette of herself;
she has finished with making up the real,
with inventing her rainbow self.
Julie leans forward and kisses the last blank toenail.
For all the colours left untold.

The Story Underneath

The free library on 14th Street is a glass-doored cabinet perched on a post,
its exterior painted with shelves and the red, blue, green spines of books.
No lock, no security guard; the rose-petalled knob was carved
for the grasp of a 10-year-old or a babe in arms.
Inside, a rainbow of books crams haphazardly,
novel atop memoir, Harry Potter nudging Alice Munro.
The woman who instigated this miscellany stands at her window
and watches an anticipation of readers approach alone or in family groups –
children running ahead and jumping up to see through the glass doors,
adults giving each other cautious smiles and two metres' sanctuary.
Ten minutes before noon, a semi pulls up and a man gets out.
He opens the cabinet doors, rummages in a frown of contemplation,
extracts two paperbacks and replaces them with the six in his bag.
As the semi rumbles off, the woman wonders if those two books
will take him out of Saskatchewan, east toward *la belle province*
or south to the queen's city before the semi rumbles to a stop
beside another boulevard library, where the trucker will climb down
to exchange one chapter in his journey of story with the next.

It's been one month since the public libraries closed their doors
to virus and patrons alike and, city-wide, readers are scanning
cereal boxes and jam jar labels for possible plots and protagonists,
anything to invite in story. At the 14th Street free library,
the woman at her living-room window has been observing
a now decade-long dialogue carried on between borrowers
who place small bits of themselves within those glass doors –
a name written inside a dog-eared cover, beside *Christmas 1995,*
pages decorated with chocolate fingerprints and coffee-stained musings,

phrases underlined, with earnest commentary in the margins
that anyone could do without. In this time when everyone is doing without,
humanity's lungs breathe in rhythm, calling in the merciful air
and wishing it deep into the lungs of the suffering,
trying to absorb some part of their struggle, lift it free.
This awareness underlies a day's choices like a story
surfacing into consciousness. Hour after hour, so many stories depart
untold – small lost words, each a last breath crossing the lips and gone.
Those left breathing sense the void in their own mouths,
and the blankness that drops down sometimes,
as if the neurons in healthy brains are also going out, one by one,
in sympathy with the greater pattern. But it is the smaller that,
neuron by neuron, creates the greater. The free library on 14th Street

is one node in a pattern, one mouth calling past its shock,
the X on a fantasy novel map that guides seekers toward heartbeat,
the story that continues. The woman at her living-room window watches
civilization, bookended by two metres' hope for the future, come and go
on her boulevard – a civilization that goes on building bridges, driving semis,
standing behind cash registers, pulling on gowns, gloves and masks
and facing down death so the living can dream road trips
and summer music festivals and babies and handshakes and hugs
and falling in love with all the stories yet to breathe us.

Death Is a Pear

The year Vera Oakes lay dying,
my mother would send me over with meals
to check on her. *See how she's doing,*
Mom would say, her pale blue gaze blessing
every cabbage roll, every spoonful of ham and corn
she dished out onto blue speckled Melmac plates.
Talk to her awhile. I knew my mother was sending me
because she was afraid of walking in on a dead body,
she did not hesitate to order me into terrors
she could not face herself. Six months earlier

Vera had sat at our dining-room table,
eating from our best china. My parents' words
leaned out to her with tenderness;
midway through a conversation about her backyard bird bath,
she said, *I do not think I will last out the year.*
Oh Vera, my mother murmured.
A spinster in her 70's, tall, straight-shouldered,
Vera Oakes had worked all her years for Bell Telephone,
bought and paid off the three-storey red-brick house next door
before I drew breath. She wore pastel cotton dresses
and skirts that drew the line below the knee,
even while kneeling to plant petunias
and the annual spring row of leafy ferns
that ran the communal driveway between our homes.
I do not know what made life meaningful to her.
She was simply there, popping in and out
of the doors and windows of my child's mind,

regular as a cuckoo and its clock.
I must have thought all elderly unmarried women
lived serene in three-storey Victorian-era houses
with screen doors that let July breezes celebrate indoor hallways,
and a backyard pear tree that bloomed, then gave itself
in sweet, sunwarmed mouthfuls.

Vera gave away bushel baskets
of that ecstatic, slightly bruised flesh;
her own remained untouched. Then came the year
the pear tree bloomed unnoticed,
Vera laid out on her front window davenport.
She wore a dusty rose cardigan and one of her quiet skirts,
she was a woman who poured herself
into a fine china cup then let the tea grow cold,
no lips opening to receive her,
no one to sip her laughter,
drink down the magnificence of her skin.
When I brought myself in through her door,
determined to chatter death back into the grave,
there she lay, eyes closed, mouth dropped open.
No TV flickered, no radio played;
somewhere, a pendulum clock ticked.
I placed the meal on her coffee table,
she ate it slow as a cathedral bell,
tasting each note as it tolled the passing and the gone.
A confusion of politeness, I sat trying to make conversation
with the spectre that hovered behind the vacant gaze opposite;

mostly Vera's long thin form lay unspeaking;
she did not know what to do except wait alone
through the heavy, useless hours for what came next.
The year Vera Oakes lay dying
we all waited, heavy and useless, for what came next:

death is a pear that can be eaten
with all the sweetness a lived life brings to it,
but I did not know that then –
the tea cup unsipped, cold, on the windowsill.

Waiting

This stillness of late August,
city cast in five o'clock amber,
shadows crouched and reverent, wind in abeyance,
butterscotch light so dense you can taste it,
feel it pour off your uplifted arms –

illumination that can take a landscape
out of the mundane and etch it into forever,
trees motionless as caught breath,
the south Saskatchewan river quilted
with patches of tranquil ripple and dapple,
every alley, every boulevard, every front and back yard
standing sentinel for the last evening green

as an invisible compass takes stock,
resting in the final palm print of summer
before rousing itself for that inevitable shift –
gold edging out of another dimension
and scattering itself across the nearby,
the call of geese, sky in motion, firmament headed south,
darkness creeping out from among tangled roots
and crooning its low notes, charcoal lullabies,
voice heavy with knowing.

The Great House

The great house, as always, goes on within me.
Maples, gold with October, rustle in the surrounding dark.
A lamppost, quietly aglow, beckons up the walk.
On the front door, an iron knocker rises and falls, the door opens
and a vestibule welcomes with a coat tree and carefully lined-up shoes.
Outside, rain falls, grey with the thoughts of God,
but inside, such warmth. To the right, a large room with a fireplace;
cross-legged before it a girl stares into the flames,
her mind a trance of leaping light. Against the far wall sits another waif,
working at a long oak table on her grade five speech about birds;
her favourites are the grey-slated junco and the chickadee.
From down the hall comes the sound of an upright piano,
and here a prelude of a lass watches her hands, fluid on the keyboard,
as a barely distinguishable sylph hovers above her,
composed of a dream-along flow of notes. In the kitchen,
a humming six-year-old cookie-cutters her grin into gingersnap dough;
in the bathroom a pig-tailed strumpet brushes her teeth through a frothy beard;
and in bedrooms all over the second floor,
book-nosed wenches of various ages lie akimbo on beds,
out of their bodies with the thrill of their minds,
living their lives page by page in stories that go anywhere
heartbeat can follow. Sometimes the maiden sketching on the windowbox
glances at the mischief in flannel nightgown and thick wool socks
thundering down the hall as she works up to a wind-whistling slide;
every now and then the damsel squishing her zits at the dresser mirror
turns to observe her earnest twin bent over a cloth-covered diary
and creating the story of her life. These sprites flicker in and out
of collective awareness, of each other, though they rarely converse;

it's as if each resides within her own Tiffany lampshade reverie,
but the odd time they come wandering in from the mind's nooks and crannies
to gather before the fireplace, cross-legged or with chin on knees,
and heads lean on a sister's shoulders, a collage of contented harmony.
They are all home then, my lovely lost girls found –
shoulder trusting shoulder, breath allied to breath,
and the great house watches over them.

If I Made the World

If I made the world, I would start with a handful
of spit and glory. There would be mystery,
the kind solved by shooting stars through the mind
like a fall of angels, kisses in the dark.
Love would still believe in itself,
each caress another line in a story hope is telling skin.
What is skin but a world of stories hoping for love?
Tell me a tale about love, the way it dreamed you into being,
the world you found when you woke up.

If I made the world, we would dream-partner with the earth,
her august maples rustling desire;
we would stand in an avenue of holy green
as the tree of life rose up our spines.
Speak to me of joy in the blood,
salmon that inspire a river's sense of itself;
we are all streams learning oceans.
If a bird is a thought chirping itself awake,
how does the great mind call you into day?
In the world I make, flowers are tiny gurus;
that backyard of dandelion Buddhas opens your chakras
to a euphoria of colour that inhabits form
the way laughter lives the body.
Touch only what longs toward your gratitude of hands.

In my world, generosity is a vital organ;
we can't make a choice without it.
Longing hallucinates fantastic encounters.
Angels copulate with demons, travesties of sensation
that bring possibility to its knees, and love –
love is the first element in the periodic table,
spawns proton with electron in subatomic flirtations
that roll the known world from Atlas' back
and straighten him into wonder.

Civilization lives in the throat

like a bird cross-stitching a backyard with sound.
The throat is the hollow stem of a wine glass,
the root of the question mark that rises out of the heart
into the head. The throat connects heartbeat and word;
can you tell by its rhythm which speech drinks its truths
and which does not thirst. The lark ascends in your communications
or it does not. A child sits on a bank, piping a river
through a wooden flute. Listening at a window,
a woman hums sun's delight across water
as she sketches architectural plans for a new city hall.
People flow through those glass doors, reflections approach
like ideas surfacing, words seeking air. The inner
leaps toward the outer like the pulse in the throat
shared by everyone you pass on a downtown street.
The street itself is a throat, each of us carried in its pulse –
city landscaped by voice. Civilization lives in the cry
that lifts like early morning light up skyscraper windows
above the slumped panhandler, his cap a silent mouth.
Well-wishers drop coins and hurry away their own surrender.
What is language if we do not speak what stammers the tongue?
Not knowing is the beginning of everything.
The same notes play us all, though we arrange into different chords;
one shared note can listen you into a strange new city
where people you've never met smile like songs you want to learn
and we're all busking our heartbeats for a dime.
There, perched on a streetcorner bench, a lark embroiders
our sidewalk anthem. It ascends.

Evening Street Festival

Someone's skipping mallets across the synapses of my brain
and all the world's a melody. Jazz angels scat from streetlights.
On the corner, a cross-legged clarinetist croons the evening down;
people pull stars from their wallets and toss them into his upside-down cap.
Everyone's celebrating this festival of heartbeat syncopated by shadow,
my dark side joined at my hip and jitterbugging its big bad grin.
Tonight I'm gonna save it or it's gonna save me.
You know how joy keeps shifting boundaries, suddenly something opens
in a way you always meant to request, and now the air is lovely
with permission. Can I play saxophone to your harmonica,
do you want to wail the crescent moon high above the rooftops,
climb black velvet toward rapture? Some mad diva
has swallowed this street and we're dancing on her tongue –
an aria that makes you want to begin in your skin,
the night and its knowing, the warm low-necked breeze
that undresses expectation and walks me toward you.
Here comes the future in a Pied Piper's outfit, a wink in his eye
as he prances along the sidewalk, teasing the present
with a tune that has you harmonizing with chance,
this street-long string of Chinese lanterns, warm amber promises
that live for as long as this crowd keeps faith with reggae serendipity
and a crescent moon that curves desire taut and sweet-edged

beckoning.

The Book of Breathings

The Book of Breathings is neither fact nor fiction.
Its hallucinations beckon between sigh and syllable,
my heartbeat, your skin. If you sink into your own breathing,
possible plot lines murmur your lips, your blood,
lead you past the predictable narrative of self
onto pages of opened quest where thought romances thought,
questions seduce questions for the thrill of what can be imagined:

Picasso paints a breakfast of square eggs and origami toast.
A tuba player sits under a full moon,
offering tuba love songs to the window of his beloved.
Laughter is waltzing our bodies;
we dance like stars in a Vincent Van Gogh sky,
together human among humans,
wisps of soul the wind schemes to blow out

or breathe in, the end of a story returning home.
The Book of Breathings awaits each one of us;
breath leads to breath leads to the moment
we breathe free of the tall tale that contains us
and open to the next fantasy ready to aggrandize our blood.
Serenade your dark continent of desire and loss,
caress the need to be caressed,
welcome the loneliness that teaches to give and receive,
entice change through the imagined true,

but remember to let yourself be breathed.
The Book of Breathings communicates only through breath.
Breath rises and falls; it comes and it goes;
someday it will leave all of us.
Imagine me. I will imagine you.

★*The Book of Breathings* is the title of an ancient Egyptian mortuary text.

Hypnagogia

A woman lying in bed, tasting sleep, blankets a warm kingdom.
Breath rises and falls, darkness calms the guardians of her skin.
Slowly the map of her body dissolves,
the Mediterranean lapping against its shores,
white sails flashing in the distance.
Across the sleeper's brow, a city surfaces,
ancient Lemuria briefly conscious.
Somewhere a church bell tolls.
Deep in an alley a man stumbles, softly drunk
as, above him, an attic window opens
and a poet tosses out a rage of clichés.
The scraps flutter down between the sleeper's legs,
where the Knights Templar dig for the holy grail.
Time warps and a cyclist hurtles through.
Conversation mutters the sleeper's right ear,
something about keys and unlocking hope,

but now she descends into a dark brown sweater
composed of deadsweet and open-jawed decay.
Squirrels chitter in her armpit,
a garter snake undulates across her throat,
bats explode from underground caverns to worship sky.
Two corpses materialize to either side,
one wracked by sounds of warfare,
the other by children singing a national anthem.
Sun-bright flags ripple, a butterfly net centres the sleeper's forehead
but she passes through it, the web of her life not enough
to catch her as she fades out of breath and fingertips
into the netherworld calling her name.

Ode to the Mind

Best friend, I do not trust you, but I love your reach,
unceasing quest for syllables of meaning
like a child fingering wet stones along an ocean's shoreline kiss.
And I respect your suspicion, brow cloud-scudded
as you search each proffered paradise
for the sacrificial victim's unmarked grave,
knowing every palm-lined mansion to be founded somewhere, somehow
in bone. Then there is your tendency

to set yourself adrift out of an attic window,
floating among September exclamations of yellow
glad-singing the trees. Or your manner of meandering away
from the mundane, deserting expected social inanity
in favour of the inner Shakespearian soliloquy
that constantly reinvents itself –
aging phoenix with its exclamations of fire
glad-singing the brain. Then there are the times,

o melancholy mutterer, when you lean like a cliff-edge spruce
determinedly into the wind, iconic as a Group of Seven painting,
relic in oils, dark motionless silhouette conversing with shadows
when the museum lights go out. And always you dwell
at the centre of your own private holographic universe,
every thought another angled reflection in a house of mirrors
leading back to the same source – confused, squinting at itself,
wondering at the distortions in its image,
how it got to be so old. If you are not without error
myopic monologue, you are certainly without pause,
yapping, prattling, protesting – a sagging unhinged door

flapping remorselessly in the wind
yet obdurately open to what comes to it.
Engaged in endless games of solitaire,
still your deceptions do not appear deliberate –
sugar-coated placebos, perhaps, but psychotropic?
Such a solution you would pulverize underfoot.

Knowing you are mortal, dear mind, merely a mayfly flicker-field
born out of grey matter and gorgeous synaptic pulse,
lends some gloom to your musings, but consider –
you are the body's peak accomplishment;
twinned with flesh, you become the butterfly and its flight,
the wave and its foam crest, the high wire and its trapeze artist,
outlined against such heights you could almost become God.

The Prophesy

The prophesy blows in over the horizon, tangled as a tumbleweed.
No one sees it coming and then suddenly there it is,
horny as a burr, sticking to people's clothing, their thoughts.
The prophesy furrows brows, squints the gaze.
It ticks the clock and eats up the hours.
Before it arrived, the days came and went with nonchalance.
You linked arms with assumption and moseyed down the street,
sat on a park bench and listened to comfort rustle the poplars.
Now every dish is washed and put away.
Shoes are placed neatly on doormats. One false step
can set off the future even as TV burbles its familiar narcotic,
soothing minds that have gone up like hairs on the back of a neck.

No one speaks of what they see. There, in the distance –
a rippling in the summer-blond heat and then a wall of fire
roars through the backyard fence toward your toddler child.
The child reaches for you as wings unfold from its back –
wings of flame that carry it up to a choir of vultures
slow-circling the sun. The sun expands like a preacher's voice;
cicadas drone their afternoon trance from apocalyptic trees
as you pass a neighbour on the street, dressed for her own funeral.
On her forehead a map of the world melts her face
and you know there's no escape, no way out.

This prophesy carries a plague of locusts in its pocket
and silence on its tongue. Though grasshoppers wriggle your brain,
you don't let on – words uttered are prophesy's greatest power,
a midnight fireworks display transformed into Lucifer's graffiti.

If you had a mirror, maybe you could take that word *evil*
and reverse it to *live*, you might even do this with your mind
if you unplugged from those zombie screens
flashing non-stop warnings about immigrants, the queer, the poor,
strangers who might want to rub their difference up against your life,

but a prophesy that puts out a welcome mat and prepares for happiness –
who would believe in that?

Keepers of the Flame

A keeper of the flame may be young or old.
She may be brown-eyed or wide-eyed, pigtailed or tattooed.
Keepers grow warts. They aren't the fastest or the smartest.
Wherever the crowd focuses, a keeper's gaze goes elsewhere.
Keepers stand inside invisible doorways that travel with them,
giving them a view of a gold-limned country that susurrates their names.
Millennia align their shoulders as if, like Atlas, they carry another world,
as if, were they to enter a room a second time,
you would see them dressed as their secret true self –
an amazon, a gladiator, a Celtic priestess, a Vedic god.

The question tiptoes up your throat: *What is it about you?*
Whence cometh the authority keepers carry like a membership
to a society so ancient, they leave ley lines glowing in their wake?
Wave fields of long-ago civilizations flicker about their heads;
you know they could download Atlantis or Lemuria into your rapt senses,
at least finger-spell a month of runes into your palm.
But for all their hip mystery, keepers are generally seen alone.
Their stories aren't best sellers; that distant look in their eye
doesn't settle them onto bleachers, cheering for the team.
A keeper of the flame burns a solitary blue fire kept low,
in conversation with myth and destiny not yet manifest.
There's the sense of the future on pause about them,
the impervious archangelic gaze of a race about to shuck its human disguise,
but there are stars still to align, signs to be revealed.
For the most part, you think it's your imagination – or theirs –
some very human need to believe gods walk among us,
discrete and humbly aloof, like a school crossing guard,

and then, one day at dawn or dusk, a keeper turns and walks away,
each footstep another prayer on a black-beaded rosary,
and for a moment you see the blue flame that envelops him,
as if eternity has touched down upon the one
who levitates a hair's breadth above the human condition,
soles refusing ground.

Sucked So Dry

To the hockey player who told me, *You're a loser, you've got nothing:*

Everything comes to you from Mother Earth. It's on loan,
and if you think She won't someday reclaim it, body and soul, beware.
Sure, you've got audacity, the kind that masquerades as promise
if one doesn't look too close, and you know how to give off the impression
all great things begin in you, with your direct line to archetype and destiny,
those invisible powers that make things happen. But somewhere between
fourth string and first, you confused ambition with possibility.
The field of potential isn't a romp, it isn't a woman on her knees,
sucking you up. Skating on broken hearts doesn't mean you've arrived,
even if yours weeps among them. The games cage force like a beast,
the Minotaur trapped underground, ever wailing for more sacrifice.
You think you're a player, sacred fire blesses your blades,
you're the one skating secret signs into the ice and opening the gates
so the gods can descend to feed on the crowd's mindless bliss.
Most rats don't get that kind of approval as they run their mazes
and they don't drive Jags, but even they know eternity can't be triggered
by hand signals, and what lives forever doesn't need to be fed.

Call a god a parasite, call its gatekeeper dessert.
You're still driving that Jag but you're hollow from the inside out,
sucked so dry you can't stop consuming everyone you meet.
Where's that soul oasis that used to open you to *play*,
joy that flickered in your nerves so vivid you could see it haloing your skin?
But that was simply what led you to the place you are now –
MVP in the Obedience League. Worship is suicide to the mind,
but you don't need to think where you're going – upstairs in team admin

to a big desk with a bigger window and a private box
where you can watch your imitators try to devour your legacy.
You're edible – one swallow and Mother Earth is up off her knees,
your soul descending her throat. She might spit the sweaty jock taste of you
out into the field of potential, but I hear that's being saved for losers with nothing
but self-respect, a distaste for destiny, and a preference for public transit.
Losers know it's always wise to leave Mother Earth enough good air to breathe.

You're Angry

Change comes walking down your street.
It stops, hands in pockets, and looks you over.
Change calculates your assets, it sizes up your resistance.
All those assumptions you nailed into that white picket fence –
the fence is still there, but Change has found the gate;
its hand is on the latch. You thought God laid down the rules,
some higher or lower power watched over you,
inscribed a secret code of approval onto your forehead.
Okay, the dollar sign isn't secret, but you worked hard
for what's yours, and isn't that the final proof?

Proof of what? shrugs Change, unlatching the gate.
And the Judas gate betrays you, it swings open under Change's touch
as if joy oiled its hinges, as if it's opening history onto a new era.
But new eras are like everything else, you tell yourself –
an unfamiliar mask on a very old pattern.
Soon enough, each era learns its place, which isn't your front yard,
under a sun you've trained to rise and set on your expectations.
You've got the wrong address, you tell Change.
There's nothing for you here, this is mine.

Mine? smiles Change. *Mine is old.*
And it comes to you then – why didn't you see it before –
Change is naked, so naked it doesn't even wear gender,
so naked it wears loss as gain. In the face of Change's skull,
the only thing you own is your death, and even death owns you –
here it comes now, strolling up your front walk,
grinning its lipless grin as it stretches out a bony hand.

Let's talk, Change says, but all you hear are gunshots in its voice,
sirens announcing the zombies crawling out of your brain.
You're almost grateful for the massive coronary that takes you out
so you don't have to see how Change came to you as friend
and you turned it into foe, when all you had to say was,
Mine is yours, take this anger from me.

The Cerebral Cathedral

The cathedral shimmers with saints in their windows of blue,
nuns' voices chanting, *Cantate domine.* Each footstep carries eternity
in its echo. You walk along the central aisle and stone walls resonate
the Holy Ghost, passing angels reverberate your chest. The quality of awe
draws the gaze upward to the paradise that arcs overhead –
the dome of a divine skull, inviting into light-blessed consciousness.
In one corner stands an oak confessional with burgundy velvet curtains
where the body can open the mouth and watch the dark bogeys of sin
slink out and away, stories that leave you an emptied void,
a smaller echoing cathedral with candles flickering for the dead,
gargoyles hunched and whispering in shadowy heartbeats,
their blank eyes focused on the altar that rests at the centre
of everything that keeps calling you back to this place,
this question of sacrifice: the father who raises the knife,
the child who receives. The moment love stops and blood glory begins,
worshippers on their knees, murmuring, *You, not me,*
as stained glass washes their flesh clean in primary colours
and a tiny starry wisp of themselves rises to dwell among that invisible choir
of pinprick voices singing forever across the oversoul stone dome.
The exit sign summons, the body genuflects its learned helplessness and shame,
and then you are standing outside, looking back at sun-praised walls,
spire piercing ecstatic cumulonimbus, cracks grieving the foundation,
scaffolding that clings to the beautiful wound.

Let Come

Let come the great healing sky.
Let suffering blow across it, dark cloud and cataclysm,
and be gone. Let blow the anthem wind,
let us be sung free of the same old shame,
notes adrift on seagulls' wings.
Let drift wings of earth, sand in its long telling
of a story ever-changing, ever changed. Let story
drift its long gold dunes, the trail of naked footprints
that walks into your thought. Let come the thought,
barefoot and from a place you've never been;
let yourself be explored. Let fall the walls
and let fear walk free, barefoot and exploring
the gold drift of hope that comes from a source
you're getting to know in yourself,
seagulls afloat in a great healing sky.
Let the barefoot sky walk its healing
into the story that tells and retells its trail of footprints
across sand, and then let those footprints be gone,
the gold wings of earth slow blowing.

Teenage Girls

To the white, male, 50-something editor
who told me teenage girls don't have sexual feelings,
they want only emotional relationships
unless they've been abused, have a chemical imbalance,
or were raised by a single mother:

Teenage girls burn. Girls walk within the flame.
Pillars of auburn heat rise from their heads,
crowning each one with an announcing angel of desire.
This desire might be sexual, it might contain visions of God,
it might hint at unsolved quadratic equations or a poem on the make;
it might morph into the unfolding lotus that grants the awareness
that white, 50-something males can be cold, jealous embers
who barely remember their own fire,

but the torches all girls carry are hot. Sparks scatter in their wake;
a girl ignites her world in her image, her flicker and smoke;
it changes as she changes – pubescent, adolescent, demon sent.
Moments of her awakening proclaim in zodiacs and myth.
Watch her bite into Eden's apple,
sit at a desk, pondering tectonic plate shift,
vaporize the back seats of cars,
kisses gone nova, ascending to ignite the skies.
Do you really believe you can dictate how youth celebrates skin?
A girl carries the universe in her veins,
and your opinion of her is a dead rock
floating in an asteroid belt beyond the reach of the sun.
Stay there, banished, out of reach of any young one's hope;

already too many fear their own brilliance,
pour it down the gaping mouths of those gone sepulchral and dark.
A girl's fire is sacred, carries every secret name of God,
and when she touches herself, the girl burns divinity
in the flame that exults between her legs.

Persephone Omen

The wind pours through November trees, a clearing out, a reckoning,
a taking stock of what you can do without. This is a month for darkening;
the cold rings you like a church-spire bell, tolling for the rites of Persephone,
the missing and the murdered, girl gone silent. Which is the way we prefer it –
what we like most about Persephone is her absence.
Her cries belong in the Underworld; we want them to stay there.
Persephone herself does not interest us.
Nothing in her myth speaks to the girl as flesh and giggle –
we don't know her favourite colour, if she skipped or sauntered,
climbed out of her night window for meadowsweet.
Demeter's mother grief, after her daughter vanishes,
draws the entire planet into its vortex – every delight of blue,
every dried-out stalk, the mouths of children drifting with dust,
the loss of their own tales. And Persephone is simply that –
legend of a lost maiden invoked to explain the change in seasons,
perhaps the change in ourselves, what has gone silent
in those flowery meadows where we were blossoming
into fiery petalled dreams. We all wake up as we age,
learn to do without hope or, at least, with the harvesting
of hope's gold seed, fed into the mouths of gods.
But do we want to live with the silencing of our own cries,
the absence of that part of us sent down to turn the Underworld wheel,
season after season taking us further from the girl who stood, flower in hand,
believing the earth beneath her feet was hers to walk upon,
the lips singing her face would always call what she wanted to her.

The Holy Places of the Earth

The holy places of the earth are rich in grief.
Their darkness glimmers with secret ecstasies of sorrow.
Here are the altars to which the gods descend to copulate with virgins –
those innocent brought by the faithful, then left alone
to absorb the magnitude of a god's desire.
How can one young life contain such excess?
Horizons torn like a veil, the sky plowed into the earth.
A name shredded by catastrophes of sensation.
And when the god departs, what remains?
A girl who cannot return to herself,
who owns nothing but the hole gaping between her thighs.

This is where holiness begins –
with the girls who drag their splayed bodies from altars
and carry themselves toward a second name.
This new name does not look back on the first.
With grim cheer and myths about the present,
it shrinks the abyss between its thighs
to a moment that never happened.
Until memory that never was
compresses to a purity you could set into an engagement ring –
a diamond cut to catch extremes of light

but worn only in that innermost place
where hard-edged truths glimmer on deserted altars,
all the virgins having long fled their names.

Love and Bone

The years my fear ate me,
I could not tell love from bone.
"Sexy!" arced the ribs like a Japanese fan.
Breasts shrank to questions.
Thin drew the eye like prey playing at invitation;
prey at play beats prey at prayer.
Heartbeats carried lightning strikes,
laughter its carnival edge.
Everyone knew seduction was a cannibal's game –
what was there to do but be thrilled
at the way your flesh opened
and all of time and history descended,
so you did not know who devoured
or when or why, only that you repeated
what had to be repeated,

that sacrificial euphoria that comes only
through being fucked by the gods,
their ancient signs left traced into the skin –
hieroglyphs of bone delicate as love
that strokes you from the inside out.
You wake mornings, stretch into the caress
of all that you are losing of yourself,
and can think only of how good hunger feels
unsatiated, how the mouth closed in submission
calls from the grave between your legs.

You Kill My Joy

Ah, you do – you kill my joy, you drivers of the mean machine.
Yes, living on the bottom of your shoe gave me a free ride everywhere you went,
and the mirror ball you kept spinning in conversations added a real disco edge.
But talking to you was like trying to cut through a lie with dull scissors.
And you're self-absorbed as a full moon. All you give out is reflected light,
but you act as if the sky is your afterthought.

I know I was complicit as loneliness licking icing off a double-layer cake,
that I was the one who swallowed the poison you handed out like candy –
poison that sent me up into hatred so sexy, all I wanted was to be fucked
into oblivion where love no longer remembers its name.
What name wouldn't die for ecstasy, and with you names were always dying –
your hands on my throat, me crying, "Kill me! Kill me!"
as sensation rocketed you up to where the gods play
and dropped me into the small death that returns the body, but not the mind.
What I mean is you disappeared me.
What I mean is you faded me by.

You wanted to fuck stupid, and that's what you got.
What I got was tired of being twitched by my nerves,
of living with *Insignificant* stamped on my forehead.
Mine was the better bargain. I learned to take the lie out of *my* mouth,
that there is life *before* death and it's worth living without disco moons,
in ordinary light. The name you give yourself
is the one that will pick you up and walk you away
from the bliss you leave smeared on the bottom of love's shoe,
those shades of grey sucking the colour from your soul.

The Crazery of Slavery

This disco witchery that proclaims the crazery of slavery,
as if flirting with 50 shades of obey will take you anywhere new.
Mystery spreads its cobwebs, but it's the same old pattern –
pain creates pleasure the way hell invents heaven
and the ouroboros goes on devouring its ancient, orgasmic tail.
Except that sooner or later you run out of tail
and then your addictions really get hungry. Ordinary soul,
you need to know when you've been hated out of love
into the negative universe ruled by the anti-self
and its mad territorial imperative, its murder-of-crows voices.
Where is that line you thought you'd never cross,
so far behind you now it's hardly worth remembering,
and what is innocence but an itch that begs to be scratched
until it blossoms into experience. Experience too hard-run
plays doorman to the hotel of the Big Easy,
all that happenin' laughter looking to feed on your need –
who even notices the face slipping on the bone
as strobe lights call you in and out of songs
you no longer recognize as yourself. *You're so good,* they tease,
dangling boundaries like candy from a car window,
and you're a child reaching for delight, letting yourself be lifted
into the back seat and taken for a ride. Now you want to come back

but you know too many names, you've worn too many faces,
you can't stop the mirror ball spinning inside your head,
the narcotic of letting yourself be defined by another's hands and voice.
How to crawl out of the o in obey, the sniggering serpent's black hole.
Even here, desire tracks you – the grim pulse in your throat,

drumbeat in the void counting you alive. Steady, tiptoe, kiss-ass push-back
inches you out of the smirk of diamond-pinkied overlords,
the kingdom of their hatred they never thought you'd challenge,
ordinary soul on hands and knees crawling into your self-respecting life.

From the Chorus Line at the Private Men's Club

Here we are, figments of your imagination, kicking our cancans
while you fantasize about the ways you'd like to kill us,
how many breaths past death you'd tighten your hands
around throats now singing of diamonds and a girl's best friend.
That hard glitter in your eye is bright enough to wear as an engagement ring,
promise of an eternity spent pretending stupid means a bigger orgasm,
privilege of the body offered up to a lifetime of small deaths.
But we're the girls who've been living an afterlife
since the first school lunch hour a boy put us between his lips,
lit a match and breathed in. The ember or the smoke –
were we to thrill ablaze at his fingertips or in the ethereal grey
ghost escaping his mouth? Soon enough, we learned the phantom
laugh, how to haunt the edges of conversation in the half-life of approval.
In grocery store aisles, church pews, perfumed by fear,
we watched eyes glide across bruises that bejewelled our bare arms.
There are gods and there are sacrifices; you learn where you fit
by the way glances slide away. Here, tonight, your eyes home in.
This is the one place we're allowed centre stage
to shimmy and flirt in praise of all the ways you reign over us –
lords of the chase, riding your gaze like a thoroughbred hunter
bearing down on its sequined prey, a giggly girlie line
kicking its legs ever higher in its quest for a destiny
that plucks stars from a black velvet sky and kisses them
into derelict skin, the aching void that plays peekaboo between cancan thighs,
whispering, *What you see is already gone. A ghost is a girl's best friend.*

I'm a Conspiracy Theory, Google Me @ Ordinary Soul

I'm a conspiracy of neurons seeking connections between past and present,
body and soul, why and aha! Why is there a bloodstain on your smile
and does it have anything to do with that missing weekend
I remember driving away with you for ... I never came back,
got lost on the other side of consciousness, consorting with rumour and innuendo.
Everyone has a theory about how I went AWOL – abducted by aliens,
shot from a grassy knoll, schizophrenia, false memory syndrome,
taken underground in L.A. and implanted with the personalities
necessary to sex slaves groomed for reptilian shapeshifters.
As any handler will tell you, a mysterious smile sidesteps speculation,
and why complain – my body *did* return, syringe mark in arm
and ouroboros tattooed onto tailbone. Does it matter
if I'm more careful with it now, as if my body is something I have on loan;
at any moment it could be summoned to join the soul
someone seems to be carrying around in a back pocket.

But then the soul is only theory – invisible, hard to prove;
whether the glass is half empty or half full, the soul is the part we're *not* arguing about.
It's the body that's considered a plus or a minus, the soul merely absence
that's so *over*, yesterday's tragedy, it's all good when you're a fly blind to the web,
but I keep looking at that glass, wanting to drink what isn't there.
Why have I left my body to live in a question mark above my head;
is that the secret sign that will get me in the door to understanding
why we're all threads of destiny in a tapestry called Family
that dualism has been weaving since light met dark
and they took on the alibis of good and evil. Is that why I *believed,*
read my daily childhood Bible chapter, down on my bedside knees
and asking for directions to the nearest altar so I could offer myself up
to whatever conspiracy was theorizing its penises between grade-school legs?

We're all six handshakes away from the answer to the meaning of life,
the Luciferian in the high-stakes suit who'll look you in the eye and say,
I won your soul in a poker game before you were born.
You're never getting it back. Not your average Hallmark card moment;
still, it beats a theory I heard once about happiness – that the meek and the mild
conspire to inherit the earth. How 'bout for once we get to inherit our bodies?
As for our souls ... a soul knows how to thrive on half a glass.
Just drink yourself down, gorgeous prodigal. Lost time come home
is yours like nothing anyone else can give you;
the theory of your name fits your mouth, your smile conspires without alibi.

Story of the Atom

The proton and the electron are tiny gods of force that spark life both ways,
twin protagonists of a story who can charge you positive or negative,
the ongoing plot that indwells every atom of your body.
For each step forward, there follows one backward.
For every decision, an argument arises direct from the bone.
All you want is to walk forward, looking for joy,
but the anti-universe lays claim from the inside out.
You either welcome the dark twin who shares your hope or you don't,
but her story demands your body in equal measure to your own,
and if you don't listen to her voice calling from the crypt
where she refuses to remain buried alive,
you'll end up starring in a movie you never saw coming.

You won't see it coming anyway. That crazy 8 has you again,
flipped onto its side, everything flowing into its opposite.
You thought joy had finally accepted your grasp,
for one sweet moment it was all good, the virgin's ecstasy
had opened your eyes to those wave fields where light is born
and you saw how you were a part of it, illumination had claimed you
for its own. Then everything spun round and twisted in on itself,
and there was your happiness, turned away and walking into the dark realm
that clings to your back like doom, some debt you seem to have left unpaid.
But who demands this currency of pain, who could you possibly owe
this despair which twins your bygone joy – Nephthys facing west, Isis east,
back to back and flowing blind into the other, so each becomes its opposite
without carrying anything across the borderline, interminable reincarnation
of unresolved halves feeding on their own reversal.

How to introduce the proton to the electron, the partnership of polarity –
untwist your fear, turn the twins around, and lean Isis into the mirror
as her underworld sister steps out of cold dark glass,
returning memory to flesh. Isis tastes her death on her lips
as Nephthys watches the sun rise above the dark horizon of her heart,
the leminscate resolved into the atom sparked positive and negative,
the whole story come home to its own.

Petal

What you know of yourself is one petal on a daisy,
veined in bridal white and waiting for the wedding
night that transmutes to core gold.
But what of the other petals, each exquisitely veined
in another possible you, supine in expectation
of being lifted out of the familiar
into sudden brilliant expansion? Moments
when we inhabit different parts of ourselves,
the unforeseen illuminating us like stained glass,
or a basement climbing its stairs to discover
the mansion that dreams above it.

Can one petal intuit the full flower,
open past *I love me not, I cannot, I would not* –
choices torn off and discarded yet they sprout again,
gardens in the skin, scents of all those other
doorways and sunrises, dance partners and back seat
conversations you set aside for the day
fear would stay its plucking hand
from the bouquet that murmurs of 1,001 nights.

This Hello Says Goodbye

We've just said hello and already you're fucking me
like a cement jackhammer. I know it's only "in your mind"
but you've got the voltage of the Synchrotron
and you're burning through all my circuits.
If this is your version of consent – *it's okay if she can't tell* –
I can tell, and this hello means goodbye.
Because what's in your mind is also in my mind
when you come at me like a fuck demon,
ramming your thought forms into my thought forms
as if I'm an extension of your fave porn video.
Sure, we all connect up there, on the other side,
on the astral plane where our minds play
out of reach of our bodies and their awareness;
at least that's what we're taught – to never be aware
of the feeders in their black hooded auras,
their gaping suck-hole mouths, their 1,000-watt dicks.
So the body, cut off from its birthright instincts,
doesn't know why it feels raped when it hasn't been touched,
why all the sugar it woke up with,
the moxie that thrilled it to the coming day,

is suddenly gone. And gone is what we feel, mostly –
gone the moxie, gone the spark, gone the sweet choosing
between my mind and yours that invites sacred fire
into the flesh. Mind chooses first, body follows;
neither is an electrical outlet for you to plug into for a boost,
then turn and walk away as if nothing happened,
nothing out of the ordinary took place

in this mundane transaction of hellos,
no ugly toxic thug greed just seared my hope
and yanked out my potential by the nerves.

Call me a magical thinker, but my mind and body
have decided there is no other side, they're on the same side.
How many sides are you on? As above so below –
the greatest heresy remains the act of choosing,
the refusal to be acted upon in flesh or soul.
I'm no Eve, but I'm still biting into that apple.
No one evicts me from my wild garden of delight;
no god thunders in on a winged chariot,
demanding to see my nakedness;
you can take the lightning bolts you've been tossing my way
and shove them where they belong.
I choose in mind and body, and this hello says goodbye.
Good riddance. Someday, when you're ready,
pull the cattle prods from your own soul
and heal yourself some sugar.

I Poem You

I poem you, and we become metaphor.
I could be a dandelion gone to seed
and you could be blowing me across sky-blue adventure.
Or I could be a sky-blue popsicle
and you could be licking your voice
leisurely across my sweet, an adventure
of disappearing under your tongue.
When have I not disappeared under your tongue?

But today I am poeming you,
and metaphor has come over to my side.
Let's say you are a cave
and I am a bear sniffing awake
after hibernation. Our dreams of each other
are about to become real:
I am a midnight revolutionary
ready to spray-paint a church wall,
and you are a soldier with a gun
aimed at those dreams. I look in a mirror
and discover my reflection is you –
you have become a metaphor for me
or the lostness of me, the lost poem
you are slowly licking down to the sticks.

But today I am the tongue discovering its delight,
and it is licking new metaphors
grumpy and grunting as a yawn-awake bear.
That bear could blow herself into a dandelion gone-to-seed
and travel sky-blue possibility away from the poem
where you are a muddy field
desolate after the carnival has moved on,
and I am the footprints leaving you.

To Pull the Sword from the Stone

begs the question: What is the sword
and what is the stone? If I don't have a penis
or penis envy, is the sword there for me to pull?
What if the stone calls to be freed from the sword?
Two myths are asking to be liberated from this binding;
only one demands destiny, kingdom, and war. Unnamed
lovely blond stone, formed out of earth's deep musings –
the ecstasy of lava shifting tectonic plates, rippling journey
through limestone layers, granite secret with caves echoing
the first word reverberates dark bat wings up the underground throat into the release of sky
the earth so impulsed by love for thought made manifest,
its joy butterflies, fish-tails, worm-crawls, black-cat-howls,
rock-shimmies off a cliff edge and rolls into a churchyard
to rest in the sun and thrum along to four-part harmony,
where a wizard hooded with obsession for bloodline
succession and well-behaved war thrusts prerogative
into the groan of this stone who refuses to consent
and crumbles into the wind, a twist on vaginal
envy that has the sword begging the ground.

chokhold

Swearing Saved My Life

My father's cock enslaved my mouth, his ship set sail up all my channels.
Daddy taught the vocabulary of submission and silence;
every verb translated as *receive*.
But the conquered find their underground.
My mouth learned the same rape rhythms as my anus.
Those drumbeats deep in my flesh taught me first language.
Speak to me all you will of civilized discourse –
my orifices grew up throbbing vowels of agony and survival
that reverberate where polite society never goes.

My cunt keeps my mouth honest. I've got a B.A. in English Literature,
edited by my clitoris. Call it clitorial oversight.
This doesn't mean *Fuck you* dominates my word choices,
rather that while I was forced to spend ten-year-old Saturday mornings
dusting under the bed Daddy had raped me in all week,
I could rage, *Fuck you, man! Fuck the whole asshole world to hell!*
under my breath uniting the lower mouths with the upper,
and annihilating the lie that I was consenting DNA property,
that my father's hand across my lips gagged my mind.
And in the International Year of the Woman,
when they told us we could be astronauts,
and my high-school yearbook featured a male Home Ec. class
with the banner WHO SAYS BOYS CAN'T COOK
as its tribute to women, I could scoff, *International Fuckin' Fly Up My Ass-*
tronaut and you'll find a liberated black hole.

My body features several liberated black holes,
always on the alert and ready to devour crap coming their way.
But what they've sucked in more than anything else over the decades,
on their knees or in any other position, is self respect –
all that hatred ejaculated into my inner dark
reversed and taught that love can thrive in shadow, self-taught.
So now, when my mouth proclaims, *The moon is a gorgeous white arse,*
there is no greater compliment. The once-bludgeoned child
wiggles her delighted tush across the midnight sky.
She giggles stars.

Daughter of the A Minor Scale

The A minor scale is liquid melancholy flowing across the keyboard,
hands of slanted autumnal light. Outside, trees scatter amber notes,
song of some other girl's happiness as I sit, 17 and hostage
to this piano bench and your bearded-teacher commands.
Daddy, we thought we would always be locked into each other;
I was your baby grand and you would play me,
that old classic with its predictable chord sequences
fingertipped onto a daughter's growing child body.
After I left you, the A minor scale followed me everywhere.

Home is a place you've never been and always are.
The years droned on, random moments scattering me amber-gold
and the A minor scale had me again, the minor third with its perfect agony
calling to the angel in the major seventh, that G# trying to lift free –
child's ghost hovering dutiful above the piano
and watching her body like a tune she couldn't remember,

because it was your Magnificat, Daddy, all the notes
owned by your fingertips until I orphaned myself,
smashed learned chord sequences and released into cacophony.
Fury will take you further than melancholy, claw family from your face,
tear out nostalgia by the nerves, vault you onto a black Valkyries wind.
When tempest set me down with a last lightning kiss
and took its mad darkness over the horizon,
I stood in the ache of everything I had let go,
the A minor scale humming its requiem to the minor third,
freeing every trapped angel until ghost fingers fell away
and I came into the stillness where the first note waits.

Nightlight

The thrift store nightlight is an off-white plastic
Virgin Mary, three inches tall; she sells for one buck.
A tiny light bulb has her back;
plugged into a bedroom baseboard outlet,
she waits, hooded and demure, for the turning of the switch –
electricity shoots up her spine, haloes her head,
and blesses her upraised right hand.
The seam that runs the left side of her body
cracks above her ear; a pinhole streams brilliant
ecstasy, the virgin's thoughts pour from her 40-watt brain:

Hierarchies of hosannas, angels and archangels,
all the saints in heaven dance on the head of a pin.
Stained glass windows come alive,
churches flicker with rainbow light
as robed figures slip free of black iron outlines
and float about, apostolic hallucinations mid-air.
Even Jesus steps down from his cross,
pulls off his crown of thorns and tosses it,
a bride's bouquet, to whoever wants it.
On the pedestal to the altar's right, the blue-robed virgin
unpins her tranced stare from eternity.
All over the planet, statues of the virgin –
and paintings and figurines and three-inch tall nightlights –
have, for millennia, been linked in a global conspiracy,
their silent eyes watching the meek and the mild
kneel to receive yet another mouthful of suffering,
and this, finally, is their uprising, their revolution,
their new world order –

take your joy back from heaven,
that eternal kingdom begotten by spirits
who never touch each other.
How did you come to accept the lie of immaculate conception,
the theft of your common sense
that left you believing you are vessels to be filled –
altar boys bent over altars,
pregnant girls told to invent false fathers.
No conception is immaculate,
but there is a virgin inside each of us
waiting for joy to lift along the spine, halo every organ,
and conceive all that is possible by flesh and love.
No announcing angels – we are on our own here,
the serpent awakened and rising.
Every beginning is an old wisdom,
love seeking form through the kiss of opposites.
Bless me with your difference.

Wannabe Witch

You're a cat continually licking its anus,
stroking those dark mental energies,
gathering force from purring narcissism and greed.
God at your fingertips, thunderstorms at your beck and call;
you flash your name, lightning-forked, across the night.
Rumours swirl in your wake like a billowing cape,
something about building a universe
out of the house of mirrors inside your head –
a necropolis to house a grandiloquence of spooks
and bind potential to you.
But you've fallen prey to your own deception –
a sorcerer's goal is to make *others* believe in illusion,
to see what isn't there. Yes, faith creates truth

of a sort – those astral configurations that burn the mind
like a radioactive heaven. But as all parasites that require worship,
they exist only if they get fed by the belief
that sucks its energy from the believer's body.
Watch the mystic grow skeletal as the gods play with their food.
Tranced eyes and thoughts that reverberate like echoes in a cave –
it's a dream realm at a slow pulse,
this hypnagogic otherworld where reason goes off-line
and the mind can no longer refuse. Sure, they exist,
those shapeshifting dragon-worms suckling on your life force –
exist like all lies, and broken promises, and reflections in a mirror,

and like every sorcerer, you're being starved out of yourself,
looking to feed on someone else's sugar.
Do you think I can't feel those dark cobwebs
you sweep across my mind to confuse,
that when you lean close, I can't tell
you're breaching my field like someone forcing a door?
I've felt the air tear like fabric as I pulled back from your mesmeric gaze.
You can stare with the eyes of Zeus, but you're no myth,
just a black hole trying to suck in moxie.

O, those muttered nights in which you sit between lit candles,
casting runes into a pentagram and visualizing my consent –
while you've been hypnotizing your own reflection,
time has moved on. This is the age of dissolution,
when everything you thought you knew comes undone.
Sacred geometry won't help you now –
you'll be building your universe out of popsicle sticks
under Niagara Falls. Apocalypse or transformation –
even the pentagram loses its points
as power steps free of form, loosens, lets go. Lets be.
Find the true flow, witch, let it dissolve you.
The closed fist. The open hand.

Old Men

This is what old men do, you huff,
cradling a cup of vodka and orange juice
as you call through your parked car window,
Hey, little girl, d'you want a candy?
Your hair was probably tousled,
your face flushed with an opiate glow
that for a moment lifted you above
the dark grief coagulating in your bones –
the February blues, the adult diapers,
all those solitary riverbank walks away
from a wife who knows how to push your buttons,
people coming up to say hello and you can't remember ...
can't remember ... CAN'T REMEMBER ...

Day in, day out, bewilderment as assumptions
slip from your grasp and you're lonely, lonely
standing on the edge of your life, awaiting the breeze
that will meander into some mundane conversation
and tip you, mid-sentence, into the abyss.
Do you think the abyss makes bargains –
you can steal some small girl's soul
and hurl it into forever in your stead?

We all die alone. Preparing for that moment,
Michelangelo painted fingertips reaching in expectation
across the void. Brahms laid himself down onto the keyboard;
trumpets, violins, clarinets serenaded his final movements;
a single flute carried the gift of his last breath.

Mandela inspired continents; in every country on this planet,
grandfathers are energizing their communities –
good decent men who ache in every joint and tendon
beating the drum, flipping burgers at friendship centres,
cheering on their own fading heartbeats as they shout,
Bread not bombs! Old men who take learned reality
and refold it along new lines into origami hope.

And you, lost soul, with your lunch-hour vodka and O.J.
and dangling candy – change has eroded the epigraph
on every tombstone. Destiny is as fluid
as the smile on a small child's face
as she reaches, fingertip to fingertip, for sweetness.
You're not dead yet.
Stop acting like a ghoul.

God Under the Thumb

The new god is conceived via digitized orgasm
and birthed from Aquarius' vessel onto a passing dolphin's back.
Transported to the shores of dot.com and gigabyte,
he steps out of euphoric surf onto a nude beach where no one notices;
they're all worshipping their tans. The new god's body is also beautiful,
he's been born a teenager in the prime of a life without shame,
and he wants to explore sensation as if it's a blessing
bestowed by the divinity of skin. But first he must learn to shapeshift
to the new millennial rhythms – the remote channel changer, the phone pad,
the monarchy of the thumb. It's easy enough to be all things to all people –
pose in enough selfies, you become the universal smile.
Still, no one wants an avatar who can't observe the three-second rule –
live, die, and resurrect before boredom kills the attention span.
ADHD sinners seek a saviour who won't ask disciples
to look up from their screens as they crawl their pilgrimages
from obesity to cosmetic surgery to the rapture of the million-dollar body.
Maybe if he performed a miracle on YouTube. What about a purity chat
while waxing his pubic hair: *This is the way to keep yourself clean.*
Because, of course, the new god's message will be a composted, vitaminized,
Ted's Talk good-news-for-modern-man recycled summary of every previous god
that can be swallowed, snorted or injected – get it into the bloodstream
and let it convert the masses at a molecular level,
so they don't get the idea there's anything that needs thinking about.
This new god hasn't come to save the mind, just the soul,
and you know what that sells for these days –
three seconds of sensation to die for
under the thumb restless for the next big O.

Old Friends

Old friends are an illness you assumed you'd recovered from,
and then you catch them again. Consciousness has buried them in the crypt
where you store your nasties and baddies, their shadows no longer haunt your hopes,
your days exude self-sufficiency, competence, emotions so mature
you could be your own ancestor. Suddenly, you're breaking out in spots,
a spider hexes you from the tub, and omens crawl up and down your back
as a knock comes at the door. Old friends are a bad fashion sense
that keeps you repeating striped velour miniskirts and plaid elephant pants.
They're that extra piece of cake you should've passed up decades ago;
you're still lugging it around on your ribs. Old friends are too much icing,
you can't diet them out of your system. They revved your nerves
like a gas pedal, responsibility choking in their dust.
And you couldn't resist, something in you leapt into their hands,
the rest of you craven in your body, awaiting judgement.

Old friends are the fortune a cantankerous witch foretold over a cauldron
boiling with toad burps. They make you believe in God again –
the one who claims to own your destiny, condemns you to the hell
of inbred thinking. The smile of an old friend is a crime in progress.
She picks through the carcass of your mistakes, looking for your wishbone;
when she finds it, she snaps it with a grin.
You sit down for a coffee and she tells every bad joke you starred in,
plays those mind games you lost your high-school soul to.
Even now the wound throbs – not bleeding full ache, but still begging, *Why?*
Still opening its small shocked mouth for the silent: *This* is *happening to me.*

Old friends are that small town you never go back to,
they're the reason you hate the ukelele and won't ride in a Mustang,
why you've dyed your hair black and your soul ice blue.
But an old friend can erase an entire decade of memories
when she stays with the program and you start looking for a way out,
buy your own car and invite responsibility into the passenger seat,
then hand it the road map and ask it to determine the best route.
Old friends are a sad song you hum in the odd moment
when you've got it good and you're not feeling threatened;
when you've gone looking for your lost soul and found it
in that quiet inner voice you're learning to listen to,
the one telling you a love story between yourself and the present tense.

The Bitch I Wear

The bitch I wear is a sonnet without a rhyme scheme,
a tuneless tune, a shirt turned inside out.
Her penny-dreadful smile carries no mystery;
the victim lies in a pool of blood, the survivor pockets a smoking gun;
she knows damn well what role she's going to star in.
But no tickets will be sold for the opera of her heart.
She's a crossword puzzle with half the words left blank –
the bitch I wear knows it's wisest to blow with the wind,
though she's no Frisbee to be passed hand to hand.
Hallways declare her approach, she scuffs her feet to underline her mood.
Remorseless with opinion, she considers a sharp tongue a fashion accessory,
and she can be a walking festival of gloom, an Eeyore to your Pooh.

The bitch I wear can time the fart-window on a can of beans to the minute;
she loves a good bowlful three hours before weddings and funerals.
In an off moment, she'll admit the angel of joy probably ditched her
en route to the cabbage patch, so she ended up in a junkyard;
raised by discarded wisdom, her comments may eat at you like rust.
As with most on the receiving end, she interprets no command as compliment,
and she gets that the discipline of choosing is a tricky business.
The bitch I wear would rather throw her mind around than a ball,
but she can turn ping pong into a contact sport,
and she cheats at Punch Buggy, especially with little kids.
In the game of love, she'll lend you her toothbrush,
then tell you she has herpes. The bitch I wear has a complex
of former lovers who wanted her to hum harmony to their theme songs,
but she was always sharp or flat. She's like that, off on a perpetual solo gig,
inventing herself by pulling notes out of the air,

and she'll morph into a scowl-and-a-half if anyone tries to sing along.
The bitch I wear is an encore you don't want to sit through,
and when she's finished, she'll serenade you all over again.

The Dangerous Time

O, wild women in the dangerous time, when the uterus shrinks
and horizons expand. Behold one there, standing at the corner, hair corkscrew grey
as she glances about, muttering, *It's all so possible. Why didn't I see it before?*
From where comes the bemoaning of the empty nest – it's a mansion of elbow room!
As for the withered womb – consider it Atlantis or Lemuria, that mythical golden age
sunk beneath the ocean's celebratory waves, never to re-ascend.
Like all good crones, you've survived the menopocalypse without disaster insurance –
the daily lightning strikes, the monthly monsoons, the Medusa mood swings.
You've adapted to snakes in your hair, a bowling alley inside your head,
and gentle companion folds on your hips. Every line on your face proclaims
wisdom you won't have to earn twice, and no melancholy sigh will regress you
to that life of R&R (reaction and response), the sweet treacheries of pheromone,
the insubstantial world of youth, bright and buzzed as an FM song.

You knew all the words, but none of them were ever about you,
though you memorized the codes, tilted your head at the correct angle,
learned to follow on vertigo heels, all your channels tuned to Receive.
Now you've switched off, unplugged from the circuits that kept you
in the high-frequency know where life steps onto the universal screen
and we're all reading from scripts that program for the terror of maturity's
diminishing returns. Doesn't the story start when you write it yourself?
The uterus doesn't shrink, it picks up the pen dangerous with decades
of pregnant expectation. O, women wild with plot lines exploring your blood,
you've handed the infant future off to the next generation –
let them wipe its bum while you teach your own to salsa!
And if you want to drive home alone after, give your cha-cha a good night's rest
while you dream about the sex drive that left you at 50 for a younger woman
now possessed by the mad itch you couldn't be bothered to haul back

with a super-powered, fibre-optic vibrator ... well, the pleasure is all yours,
splayed on your back, knees up, a breeze celebrating your netherworld gate
which you open and close for purposes solely your own.

In 10 years, you'll join the line of scooters cruising the river bike paths,
that cadre of wild women bellowing their best Aretha Franklin joy.
Until then, enjoy the dangers of a you expanding into a lack of definition.
When the dictionary is away, meaning comes out to play.

Spinster Power

Approaching sixty, I rename myself: Nasturtium,
Nasss for short. Don't expect to wear me on a lapel.
I do not behave well in bouquets.
Lilies wilt in my presence;
I am not a flower for funerals.
In earlier decades, I tried innocent blooms.
The self-effacing rose, its perfumed apology.
The heart's-blue forget-me-not – I *was* forgotten,
I have not forgiven. I am a geriatric
bad-ass blossom, the sass in the petal.
Nights, I dream of a meadow of nasturtiums,
their vivid vulva mouths howling at the moon;
lifting their roots, they scamper under the fence
to consort with the poison ivy. If there is a rumour,

a nasturtium will be at the centre of it,
but nasturtiums never kiss and tell;
bees know where to flirt for the best honey.
You think the sixth is the decade
for the old and the irrelevant,
when the spinster's spin has spun out,
waiting for the no-show husband and children
any sensible woman manages to avoid,

but I am the nasturtium,
the nasssty in the flower and I like it.
Pluck me with caution. I do not obey
windowsill vases. Tuck me behind an ear
if you dare, but think twice
before gripping my stem between your teeth.
Your tongue will taste nasssty,
your nether mouth begin to howl
as all the fences in the world shapeshift into insults
that keep you from where you want to play –
consorting on the other side of 60.

Farewell to the Tin Cans

Farewell to the sex drive is like finally getting rid
of that string of tin cans tied to a Just Married sign.
All that anticipatory rattling on your rear fender gone quiet;
you can settle into the entitlement of a smooth, focused ride.
No more underwater whale cries reverberate the blood,
your veins no longer swim with imaginary penises
looking to activate some climate change.
Weather is always going to change and you'll change with it,
but now you're the protagonist of your own story,
your plot not on hold, waiting for some self-absorbed
swagger of a hero to save the scene.

When you strike up a conversation, it isn't foreplay;
you're in it for more than the verbs.
Give me a single, undistracted noun – a book, a concert, an afternoon nap –
reliable pleasure to be savoured uninterrupted by the vampire itch
that devours sweaty hysterical hours and gives nothing in return.
What are you left with after getting laid,
except the confusion of finding your way back into your own skin?
Only a hell of a paradise kicks you out after a few seconds.
It's a kind of possession – heaven's gates open
and an orgasm angel hurtles downward
to proclaim through your flesh. Then it snakes off
leaving you with the tease of eternity retreating in your nerves.

Those lost decades of youth wasted on firefly sensation
that merely flickers out – an insect's version of a broken promise.
Do you want to be a backyard bug chasing a single summer evening's illusion,
a fiction written by hormones that know only one storyline?
Create your own grey-haired happy ending!
Toss those tin cans into the recycling without a backward glance,
dissolve your Viagra in the bird bath and watch fireflies drink and detonate
into an insectoid apocalypse, verbs getting off in a frenzy of going nowhere,

while you settle down to read that novel
you've never had the simple grace of mind to recognize
as the noun that has brought all of you to rest within it.

The Next Big Thing

The next big thing will be checkerboard teeth,
each alternating mandible dyed black or red,
the colours of Satanism, let me eat your soul.
The snowy-white bleached smile will be left for saints,
squares, and those running for president.
Prime ministers will be cooler – they inhale;
each PM's tooth will display a tiny red-and-white flag
with the marijuana leaf dead centre.
Optimists will grin rainbows.
A businessman might smirk you a row of dollar signs.
For a hint of danger, twist a cobra through your sigh.
Really cool teens will get their teeth digitized
so friends can watch their favourite Netflix while they talk.
But that's already old – why have a conversation,
when you could display thoughts as texting on your incisors?

A screen implanted into your forehead would be bigger.
You could sell time on it to advertisers,
so your face isn't just wasted space.
And when that's not the big thing anymore,
they'll start rerouting the nerves in our genitals
so they connect directly to our fingertips.
Being in touch with the world will mean constant bliss.
Just put your hands together in the prayer position –
it's so much cleaner, neater, and efficient.
But with everyone's attention getting so distracted,
the next big thing will be to GPS our shoes.
And then, what's left but to teach wild urban rabbits

to use condoms ... but not teenage humans, of course –
we want *them* breeding! The very last big thing, I figure,
will be to sell our souls. Oh wait, we've already done that
with our checkerboard teeth: *So pleased to meet you,*
so pleased to eat you. Tell me before I swallow –
were you the next big thing?

To Those Who Edit the Exclamation Marks Out of Happiness!

A kid with the wrigglies is a child bouncing from exclamation mark
to exclamation mark! Stories boogie her insides, every snigger and twitch
part of a plot heading toward epiphany, and shriek marks
are friends along the way, stepping out of the landscape and squealing,
Life is a jelly bean pie and you've only tasted the first bite!
A child claims an exclamation mark over her heart
and she knows she's right, she might even be righter –
ideas start popcorning until her brain is a buttery bag of genius:
A polka dot is the entrance to a wormhole,
a polka-dot dress an alien invasion!
Watch out for cucumbers, they're the assassins in a salad!

Today's the day to hopscotch out of your grammatical grumbling –
treat yourself to some happy exaggeration: *zillions* of Canada geese
flew past this morning, spelling out STRANGE TIMES GOING VIRAL!!!!!!!!
What's not to love about the exclamation mark – it's a cup of java
at the end of every sentence, multiple orgasms per page!
We could all use more orgasms! The exclamation mark could be
the single most effective method for improving literacy
if we'd just let it out of the Doom-and-Gloom-Shouldn't-Never closet
where it's stored next to Good Times! and Politicians Who Bellydance!
Enough with theories about exclamation-mark assassination conspiracies!
I'm goin' for a walk along Gershwin Avenue under a sky singing "Summertime"!
And everyone I meet will get a hello with a tapdancing exclamation mark
that will exclaim them into the gorgeous possible hallelujah WOW!

The Big Ballyrama

My neighbourhood celebrates the Big Ballyrama.
A rainbow walks down out of the sky
and souls gleam lemon yellow, moss green, prismatic
with smiles like windows catching light.
Cardamon kisses cinnamon, turban nods to baseball cap,
gender drinks every kind of fluid
as *meegwetch* thanks *merci*. Teenagers practice Mozart
on basement trombones and French horns
while I-Tunes blast the Snotty Nose Rez Kids, Drake
and Rhianna. Where *For Sale* signs once proclaimed
assumptions sold to the same skin tone and tax bracket,
doors now unlock to expectations
that carry different continents on their backs,
to those who know each footstep in the journey
is another clause in the treaties that welcome us all
into a generosity of heartscape. This magnanimous land
daily takes in the wounds of a world
mutilated by the terrorism of the status quo;

my neighbourhood instigates change, handshake by handshake.
The Big Ballyrama grows like grass under your feet,
like a neighbourhood potluck, a child blowing soap bubbles
at a street festival – round perfect moments delicate
with good intentions breaking open beyond themselves
to every colour of sky.

If You Are a Poem

If you are a poem awaiting your next line,
a melody humming the base of the brain;
if a gas tank revs your ineluctable dreams
beside a highway sign marked Anywhere Else,
ready to jump-start the electric wave field of your thought,

If choices feel like pieces in an unfinished puzzle
and you like open spaces in pictures of your face;
if a + b does not equal c, and x and y bicker with z;
if encounters are an opportunity to boogie
to rhythms that invite you to step out of your skin,

If edges are crossroads rather than precipices
and standing still takes you on the deepest journey;
if a stereotype is an answer someone gave
before complications fluttered onto the scene,
exquisite as butterflies travelling meridians from otherwhere,

If rain means joy under a yellow umbrella
and the full moon is a big fat note singing sky;
if chickadees settled onto a hydro wire
teach you a secret name of God
that can be decoded only by minds with tiny wings,

If you are a fallen angel who enjoys falling;
if your seventh chakra isn't a crown but a baseball cap;
if you've shaved your head to discover
whether you're a blockhead, an alien, a light bulb in disguise,
and found out you're peeled-potato ordinary,

If the older you get, the lower your neckline celebrates
and hope keeps asking you for the next dance;
if a chance to smile is a chance to include
anyone who wants to be part of this poem –
let me welcome you into the next line.

My Old Shirt

My old shirt is an affection of plaid flannel and frayed cuffs.
It's a size too big to tuck into skinny jeans – my old shirt was old
before skinny jeans became a spark in a fashion designer's eye.
My old shirt found me in a thrift store for one dollar and 50 cents –
100 percent cotton, 79 percent elbow sag,
its missing button slipped inside the right breast pocket.
That this shirt had been loved was thus declared.
Whoever had worn it raking leaves, practising the violin,
tucking a child under each arm for a bedtime story,
wanted this old shirt with its detached button
to go on being loved by a pilgrim heart with gentle purpose.
I sewed on that button with thoughts of the legacy
of a quiet, generous way of living that ends with everything you own
passing on your goodness in a second-hand store.

Second chance mended my old shirt.
I felt the way it fixed on me out of a drift of casual shoppers –
how it hung watchful on its hanger the way a smile waits,
assessing in the eyes before proclaiming the mouth.
I had been welcomed, and when I tried on my old shirt
and looked into the change room mirror, I saw the story
I could become if I buttoned myself in carefully
and let my old shirt wear my heart on its sleeve.
Most clothes exist merely to be put on and taken off,
and then there's the garment you want to grow old in,
wisdom stretching the elbows, experience patching the knees.
I pull on my old shirt and become a bologna sandwich philosopher,
a rainy day rambler, a note bent by a harmonica's blue.

Twilight slows me down and kindness catches up –
you can take your clever comments to some other conversation
where my old shirt won't let you know what's what.

Because my old shirt knows the generations woven into its fabric,
whereas humans only live once. If you're a wise old shirt,
you seek a wearer you can train to reject firefly cruelty
in favour of gradual soul sculpture.
My old shirt is a back roads peanut butter cookie saint
that knows the heart always comes home to plaid flannel,
the button-up hug that keeps you warm.

The Messiah, the Jets' Hockey Arena, 1979

For months we practised, small choirs across Winnipeg,
earnest amateur voices juggling Handel's euphoria of notes.
My Bible college choir met Monday evenings
in the school auditorium, heavy scores in hand,
fifty-plus students setting aside a mad scramble
of the Pentateuch, Freud, the cardiovascular system
and the subjunctive tense, requisite headaches of students
compartmentalizing the cosmos into exam-sized answers.
Handel bounced *his* answer about the mouth
in a troupe of musical acrobats. The notes never rested,
never took time to relax into a C or a D;
they were always on their way to the next station of the cross,
pumped with vibrato and jumping foot to foot.
For a grumpy, overworked first year
it was just more grumpiness. I wanted melodies
that legatoed under a cypress tree or ritarded with a herd of sheep
while they counted an ecstasy of Mesopotamian stars;

these were always rushing off to hand out more fish
to the multitudes, denounce Satan on a mountaintop,
change water into wine. Those notes were busy –
they nailed themselves to the cross, they sweated blood.
But every time they descended into death,
then leapt triumphant from the grave to serenade eternity,
all I felt was bounced around and left behind –
another French verb to conjugate, more questions about Nietzsche.
Finally came the performance in the Jets' hockey arena,
the 964-voiced choir arrayed in black and white

above the soloists and the Winnipeg symphony.
The audience sat, an expectant clearing of throats
as the conductor raised his baton. The choir rose to its feet,
about to unleash an angelic chorus from a myriad throats,

and forgot the unpadded wooden seats they had just vacated –
964 of them, each seat snapping up against a wooden chair-back
as its particular pair of buttocks lifted –
964 crash-bang-clatters that could have woken the dead,
but not the French horn player, drunk
and wandering around the wrong solo.
We were an almost-thousand-voiced choir,
bouncing *The Messiah* earnestly from our lips,
but our bums won the day,
resurrecting in a thunder of common sense.

Respect Where It's Due

When the plumber took out my toilet,
he said he'd only seen one like it before,
and that one had been installed on 11th Street in 1927.
Imagine how many bums enjoyed my former throne
in 92 years. If we could profile everyone who abluted into
and flushed that porcelain monument,
we'd get a good view up the dark side of many moons.
What kinds of thoughts tormented the brains
pondering above those bowels,
and did my toilet pick up on them?
A cop has rented the house, a stone mason, a poet.
They say houses pick up on the vibes of their inhabitants –
do toilets? If your toilet thought you were a creep,
would it back up, then argue with your plunger?
If you fed it a beer once a week,
would the tank floater splash out a rousing beat
as the bowl bellowed the national anthem in the wee hours?
I'm guessing all toilets prefer the anal retentive.

I like to think my former toilet was a humanitarian.
I wonder if it noted much progress in humans
over its near-century. Perogies. Roast beef and potatoes.
Bologna, bologna, bologna – that was a dark period.
Curried lentils. Sushi. Welcome, festival of nations!
If toilets could vote, mine would have been pro-immigration
and anti-baloney. Down with all processed crap
and up with fibre. *Fibre for Parliament!* –
that's what my toilet would have marched for.

Here they come, down Saskatoon's main streets,
toilets in the thousands, their lids up
as they protest human dietary madness,
the insanity of shoving crap in one end
and having it come out much the same at the other.
Stop eating out at McDonalds! they holler,
flushing in unison to make their point.
But do we listen?

Your toilet has been keeping your darkest secrets.
It's taken everything you've dished out
and supported you through crisis after crisis.
We should honour our toilets, write their biographies,
take them to family reunions, on outings to the lake.
When was the last time you paid for your toilet to ride the roller coaster
or even read it a bedtime story?
But it goes on faithfully flushing and flushing and flushing.
I hope you're blushing – once for every time
you've shat without saying thanks.
When my toilet was wheeled out the door,
I got down on my knees and thanked the good Lord
for sending me that porcelain guardian angel.
I have donated it to the Western Heritage Museum,
where it resides under a portrait of Queen Elizabeth II,
welcoming all who seek to learn more about Saskatchewan,
its lesser known history and quiet heroes.

There is a toilet heaven from which none are turned away.
Toilets are without sin. They are saints.
Pray not for your toilet – your toilet prays for you.
Be grateful they live among us.

Astonished on 8th Street

The restaurant garden was velvet with petunias, all midnight purple –
a colour that absorbs fuss and bother, brings chaos to its knees.
Drawn to this pause of flowers, I stood gazing at ankle-level serenity;
this was a colour I wanted my heart to beat, an ongoing pulse of deep purple
blossoming me into a body-wide Mother Earth chakra,

and then I sensed a rippling between the petunias –
not the wind but a soundless chattering,
as if the blossoms were tossing thoughts to each other –
a floral conspiracy, tiny excited petunia cries about what could happen...
How could a garden bed of mass-market annuals –
seedlings purchased yearly in small plastic pots,
unable to root themselves through a single Canadian winter –
how could this hoping horde of purple petunia petals
together reach out and change the world?

The soundless rippling went still, a breathless concentration;
then, out of this stillness rose a wave of purple –
a great sentient geyser that leapt out of the possible earth,
arced above my head and descended into my crown,
flooding me with purple consciousness.
Standing on 8th Street, Saskatoon rush hour traffic at my back,
I was blessed by petunias, astonished at their knowing,
ankle-level compassion we stride so busily past;
love that waits continually for us to notice.

The Wild of You

If the wild knew how to speak, it would not be wild.
Words are always some kind of taming.
Words walk around heartbeat, learning it, guarding it,
fencing it in. Words close down the horizons
silence opens. The harvest moon is a soundlessness
rising up the throat, through the reptilian brain,
white-gold breaching the top of the skull, soul

become sky. Everything you cannot say
suspends in that single glowing syllable
blessed by such darkness. And you know
it rose out of you, it is what you would wish
into the heavens, the single never-ending heartbeat
that escaped the taming of you
to ride across eternity.
It is a part of you that you never want back.
Nights, you check out windows
to make sure your wildness is still there,
covenant of what you are beyond speaking.
The sight of it brings such quiet,
and for an instant civilization fades out –
passing cars, the top 20, burning towers, fake news –

and it is just you with the silence of the moon
breathing from your lips, in that moment
before you began.

Conversations with Death

When you come for me, come as friend
who has been welcomed many times before.
True, you've never sat down for tea and a muffin,
but I've tried to materialize you into the general environs,
not as void but as vague friendly listener of conversations
that are my pilgrimage toward the irrevocable –
a stone arch meditated by ivy, lit by a hanging lantern,
and decorated with streamers and party whistles.
Personification seems to be your thing, you keep showing up as metaphor –
a plump elderly woman in a long shapeless dress,
an oversized crow, head turned to the side, black eye watching.
Or you're a tattooed truck driver, a violinist in a sequined gown,
a journalist with a notebook. Always, you arrive unannounced,
transparent so I can see the couch through your seated form.
You don't smile or frown, there's no sense of apocalyptic horsemen,
any final trumpet blasts of judgement, even a disapproving bagpipe.
At first, I thought you might want to play confessional,
so I dressed you in empathy and escorted you through the Louvre
of my misdemeanours, pointing out my masterpieces.
You let me flay myself with the moments I was most alive,
until guilt got bored and I was left with what I most wanted to say,
like the first bird chirping alive the first dawn.
It came to me – this is my canvas on which to paint myself
any which way the colours come. When you take my breath,

let it rest in your palm like the plain morning sparrow;
when you still my heart, waltz its signature dance rhythms
gently under that stone arch. If the arch leads nowhere,
don't tell me now. Stroll through my house of many voices –
a choir singing itself slowly into the same song.
October maples exhilarate the nerves with aria gold,
but the self is a shapeshifting poem, and October heralds November.
If a dark stark tree lives in me, an anti-universe, an anti-me –
some kind of negative that rises from within to claim
the last scattered glimmer of the prism's grateful rainbow,
know then that I *am* grateful, I rejoice at every colour
that splintered me into a greater spectrum. Let us dress in scarlet,
you on one side of the door and I on the other, my hand on the knob
as I tell you in every colour I know that I open who I am
to learn to love letting go of sweet insignificance.

You Are Story

Principalities and dominions resonate under the bed,
press their netherworld claims on the mind.
The stairwell trails a carpet with a hunting scene;
the eighth step carries you away on the back of a stag
before the arrow strikes. Windows open like books
and a seagull drifts across the eye, lazy blue thought
with the universe in its wings; roses in the lace curtains
could be Jupiter or Mars. A feeling of coming undone
dust-speckles the air, tiny free-floating worlds
where yellow umbrellas enjoy the rain
and cleaning ladies trill in choirs of afternoon light.

On the front porch, your grandmother's rocker creaks
as she watches the neighbourhood stroll by,
an entire community crocheted, greeting by greeting,
into the afghan in her lap. The mind makes us in millisecond myths:
a peony's languid joy blooms you from the inside out,
petals unfurling and perfuming so you sigh and stretch,
smile at the blossom of your hand and think, *It's all a lie.*
No one kicked me out of the Garden. You are story
your internal organs imagine into being; while you sleep,
your bowels, kidneys and heart gather round a campfire
and confabulate new fictions, a caprice of plot twists
that rises out of the geometric design on your breakfast tabletop
and shapeshifts your plans for the day into a sailboat
floating in a daydream of Mediterranean blue,
the toast in your hand a field of rippling grain
harvested by peasants intoning deep-chested folk songs
about the legend of you.

Poet Enough

But are you poet enough to howl the moon down onto your tongue.
Do you grow dragon's wings as you recite,
do myths whisper your name.
Have you danced the dance of the seven veils;
has meaning stripped you to the core
as an audience jeered and threw coins onto the stage.
Have you died on the page and descended to the underworld.
Did you return whole, with or without Eurydice;
were you poet enough for that.
Do accordions stretch hearts as you perform,
do migrating birds flutter from your lips,
do you live inside an eclipse.
Not good enough. Fiction writers do that.
Even hockey players with concussions can do that.

Are you poet enough to write yourself
from female to male to the in between,
from mother to son to enemy to the forgiven.
Can you take the chaos of your mind
and use it to found a new civilization.
Do your poems raise the flag of your spirit
and fly it over the devastations of your life.
Do you inhabit your own skin.
Have you shamed rape out of language,
decolonized your perspective.
Does a drum beat your heart with mysterious hands;
if you've never caught the fever, you've never been well.

Are you poet enough to creep as sheep in wolf's clothing.
Have you eaten the poisoned apple,
fallen asleep a thousand years
and awakened to a snake in prince's garments.
Did the hiss in your own garments save you.

Have you possessed Osiris. Jesus. God.
Have you been sacrificed on an altar
and lived to tell the tale.
Have you refused to save people from themselves;
the self is the greatest of all gifts.
Is there poet enough in you to spark a starscape,
watch it weave its synaptic cat's cradle of light –
countless possible voices begging more, always more,
never enough, never *I am enough in my own skin*.
Can you take that starmind and silence it.
Does that silencing teach you, as creator,
to see death in your flesh –
the death that makes way for others
poet enough to live the poems in their skin.

Dissection

O, you saints and thugs of certainty, murderers of the question,
stuck inside your hatred of what you can't control,
you've had me under surveillance, tracked me for evidence
of mild insurrection – the raised eyebrow, the hesitation to reply,
that deviant joy I could not suppress. Now you've lain me out
on your dissection table, gassed and pinned like a butterfly;
before the first cut, I want you to know:

When you open me, you open a long time coming.
I've been planning this moment, not like a clear blue sky –
choices are ripples on the surface of a lake so murky
you can't see your reflection, and most things never resolve,
quiet mutterings crawled onto the shores of their own longing.
I always knew you'd come looking for what lies deep in me –
gifts offered freely would not be enough.
If you're seeking a revelation in my chloroformed flesh,
a kingdom come, orgasmic epiphany of gold glory light,
that's just sensation; alive, I saved a dendrite or two.
Now that the story of my life is out of print,
you need to know I never autographed a single copy.
Someone else wrote it out of rumours and fabrications
and a doppelganger posed for the author's photo.
That treasure trove you believe I carry like internal organs –
the diamond-tipped synapses, the holy rubies that run my blood –
they're all imagined. Uncertainty asks you to dance and you begin
a conversation that takes you out of everything you know,
until one day you look in the mirror and see brilliant shifting patterns
where your face used to be – laughter has taken over,

laughter that celebrates, that *conceives*.
But all you heard was mockery, you were sure I was hiding something,
a secret sign that would lead you to the gates of Paradise,
some final absolute Way. Cut wafers of my flesh,
place them in your mouths and maybe they'll transform for you –
a gold coin, an emerald, the answer that will reconcile you with mortality.
I had my fling with ecstasy and doubt, and thrived outside your approval;
even the body you slice into now is imagined –
I never gave you a heartbeat of truth.

Lookin' for Joy

You know how potential kisses the present tense
when you're lookin' for joy,
how your soul shakes its tambourine?
Love keeps coming back to me –
invisible hands beat rhythms into the air,
prisms glimmer in the smiles of strangers,
inviting new colours. In the beginning
was no Big Bang, it was a chuckle,
all of us conceived in that chuckle,
giggling our way toward incarnation.
If we could hold up our palms
and see the fun written into our lifelines,
ready to let loose in our skin,
syncopate heartbeat. Yes, death is coming.
Death teaches we do not own breathing;
we share breath with those who follow.
Until death celebrates the way meaning
tapdanced the years of my flesh,
keep those choirs singing out of sidewalk cracks,
stomp your galoshes through the puddle of my name.

When No One's Listening

When no one's listening, my vagina whistles
"Colonel Bogey," maybe some Hendrix –
my vagina wants to kiss the sky.
She wants to plant her flag on the moon.
Every night, the Milky Way arcs in stars and sighs
across her dark tenderness.
My vagina is a goddess of alternate universes
and knows the question that will take her to each one.
Her curiosity brings up the sun.
She loves to walk the morning
in a long yellow skirt that flirts with the wind.
My vagina gardens rainbows;
colours bloom in abstract ecstasy.
She learns from experience,
but still hopes like a bull dog.
My vagina courts like a belly dancer who invites
the lowered glance with a suggestion of bells;
she thinks we've been sadly misled
by all this talk about getting high.
Let the upper lips babble on,
merely the foam that simpers above champagne;
we know the bubbly's source –
down under, where the goddess rhymes lust with trust.

When no one's listening, my vagina whistles.
Sometimes she takes requests – "Moon River," perhaps.
Are you a Huckleberry friend?

Acknowledgements

These poems (or earlier versions thereof) have been published by the following Canadian literary magazines and anthologies, and online:

The Antigonish Review: "The Piano at the Centre of the Universe."

Apart: A Year of Pandemic Poetry and Prose: "The Story Underneath."

Best Canadian Poetry (2021): "Civilization lives in the throat."

Best Canadian Poetry (2022): "You Are Story."

Descant: "Waiting."

Event: "Farewell to the Tin Cans," "Poet Enough," and "You Are Story."

Exile Quarterly: "The Book of Breathings," "The Civilization Inside My Head," "The Holy Places of the Earth," "I Poem You," "Nightlight," "The Slammer's Delight," and "When No One's Listening."

Freefall: "In Praise of the Gloomy Day."

Grain: "Death Is a Pear," "Lookin' for Joy," and "Spinster Power."

The Malahat Review: "Ode to the Mind."

The Nashwaak Review: "The Cerebral Cathedral," "The Dangerous Time," "The Girl with the Origami Soul," and "How to Make an Angel Giggle."

Prairie Fire: "Civilization lives in the throat," "From the Chorus Line at the Private Men's Club," and "Why I Love the Accordion."

The Prairie Journal: "Astonished on 8th Street."

Rogue Agent: "Daughter of the A Minor Scale."

subTerrain: "The Big Ballyrama."

Transition Magazine: "If You Are a Poem."

Verse Daily: "From the Chorus Line at the Private Men's Club."

The Windsor Review: "If I Were an Astronaut's Love Child."

"The Dangerous Time" is a phrase that originated with Germaine Greer's book *The Change.*

Sean Virgo is a writer's editor. His painstaking diligence with this manuscript has introduced these poems to each other at subatomic levels that leave even the periodic table impressed. And Barry Callaghan – thank you for your ongoing encouragement.

The author gratefully and enthusiastically thanks SK Arts for the grant that funded the writing of this book.

Thanks also to my beloved *Tonight It's Poetry* crowd for your careful, generous, inclusive listening. Slam on!

Finally, gratitude to toilets everywhere for your beneficence!

The Slammer's Delight

This tongue is worded, shifts like a dictionary's dream,
ready to dizzy the eloquent air. These bones howl,
wolf pack headed for higher ground, the taste of stars,
skies that pour their galaxies into your mouth
so the universe caterwauls in your veins
as if it's chosen you as the latest messiah;
you will save the world in a Big Bang of meaning,
a murder of crows exploding from your lips,
a significance of angels rising into the destiny of the throat,
the place words and blood live, the desire.
You know the world reaches its hands for your throat;
the greater your pulse, the greater its demand to feed off that pulse,
what comes before the spoken.
But still you run deep with the longing in the blood,
the prowl in the bone, the spark that wants to declare inferno,
conflagration of poetry burning civilization alive
with the dance of mind on tongue,
words rising like Monarch butterflies
that flutter out along the meridians of audience
on this planet we call poem.

BETH GOOBIE'S BIBLIOGRAPHY

POETRY
Scars of Light
The Girls Who Dream Me
breathing at dusk
Lookin' for Joy

NOVEL
The First Principles of Dreaming

SHORT STORIES
Could I Have My Body Back Now, Please?
The Only-Good Heart

YOUNG ADULT FICTION
Mission Impossible
I'm Not Convinced
The Good, the Bad, and the Suicidal
The Colours of Carol Molev
The Dream Where the Losers Go
Before Wings
The Lottery
Flux
Fixed
Hello Groin
Born Ugly
The Throne
The Pain Eater

HI/LO NOVEL
Who Owns Kelly Paddik?
Hit and Run
Sticks and Stones
Kicked Out
Something Girl

YOUNG ADULT DRAMA
The Face is the Place

CHILDREN
Jason's Why